The World of Nature in the Works of Federico García Lorca

edited by
Joseph W. Zdenek

ISBN 0-933040-01-6

Copyright: 1980
Winthrop Studies on Major
Modern Writers

General Editors:
Lawrence D. Joiner,
Earl J. Wilcox,
Joseph W. Zdenek

PREFACE

In May, 1978, the first Winthrop Symposium on Major Modern Writers was held on the campus of Winthrop College, Rock Hill, South Carolina. One of the fruits of the proceedings was a volume of essays chosen from the papers presented by scholars from every region of the United States on the theme, "The Art of the Proustian Novel Reconsidered."

This is the second volume of the series, containing selected papers from the second Winthrop Symposium on Major Modern Writers, held in May, 1979, which had as its theme, "The World of Nature in the Works of Federico García Lorca." Again the essays include contributions of young scholars of García Lorca as well as established ones.

The 1979 Symposium could not have been a success without the support and help provided by Lawrence D. Joiner, Dean of Continuing Education, and his staff at Joynes Center, the administration of Winthrop College, and all the participants of the Symposium. Thanks also go to Lorraine Gorrell, Gregg Hill and Dean Jess Casey of the Winthrop School of Music for providing a fine evening of songs by García Lorca and de Falla.

We anticipate that this second volume will be followed each year by another dedicated to literary scholarship.

Joseph W. Zdenek Winthrop College

CONTENTS

GUSTAVO CORREA   1
    The Mythification of Nature in the Poetry of
    Federico García Lorca

MICHAEL J. FLYS   19
    The Changing View of Nature in Federico García Lorca

CANDELAS S. NEWTON   29
    Two Aspects of Nature in *Libro de poemas:* Nature
    as the Lost Paradise and Nature as Teacher

ROBERT TER HORST   43
    Nature Against Nature in *Yerma*

DAVID K. LOUGHRAN   55
    Imagery of Nature and its Function in Lorca's
    Poetic Drama: "Reyerta" and *Bodas de sangre*

RUTH AYÉNDEZ-ALDER   63
    Imagery and Theme in *El Maleficio de la mariposa*

MARIE-LISE GAZARIAN-GAUTIER   73
    Doors and Windows as a Luring Call of Nature
    in the Work of Federico García Lorca

BONNIE SHANNON McSORLEY   81
    Nature's Sensual and Sexual Aspects in Three
    Gypsy Ballads of García Lorca

JAMES E. LARKINS   91
    The Mythical Aspect of Death in the Natural
    World of the *Romancero gitano*

HARRIET S. TURNER 101
    Circularity and Closure in Lorca's Trilogy

FLORENCE L. YUDEN 117
    The Yes and No of Lorca's Ocean

BARRY E. WEINGARTEN 129
    Bernarda Alba: Nature as Unnatural

MARÍA TERESA BABÍN 139
    The Voice of Nature in the Life of the Water
    (García Lorca's Vision from 1923 to 1936)

THE MYTHIFICATION OF NATURE IN THE POETRY OF FEDERICO GARCÍA LORCA

Federico García Lorca was a poet of nature. He was born in a small Andalusian town, near the city of Granada, and was surrounded by nature and steeped in it from his early childhood. His background was essentially a rural one. This means that the dawning of his consciousness as a poet took place in a constant and intimate communication with nature. His first vocabulary and mental outlook in the understanding of the world had to do with the people, the objects, the smells, colors and sounds of the rural landscape in the countryside of Granada. This first contact of the poet with nature will always be present through his poetry, whether he is exploring the mystery of his own self or of the universe, or delving into the dark forces of nature and man, or trying to face the enigma of human destiny. The poet himself has dwelt on the importance that this early communication with nature had for him. In an interview published in his *Obras completas,* he has the following to say of his early childhood: "When I was a child I lived in an environment which was completely saturated with nature. As all children do, I used to give to every single thing, to every piece of furniture, to every object, tree, rock, their own personality. I used to converse with them and I loved them."[1] And also: "I love the land. I feel that I am intimately tied to it, in all my emotions. My farthest recollections from my childhood have the taste of the land. The land, the countryside, have done great things in my life. The tiniest creatures of the earth, the animals, the country people, all of them have for me hints and suggestions that do not have for other people. I feel them now with the same spirit with which I felt them in my childhood years. Indeed, if it were not so, I would not have been able to write *Blood Wedding*" (p. 1755). Nature, thus, acted for Lorca from the very beginning, as a kind of a primary code in the awakening of his poetic consciousness. It constituted a path for the structuring of his mental development and set the trajectory for the formulation of his emotional life. This absorption of nature by the poetic consciousness in its formative years is no doubt a key to the powerful appeal that the poetry of Lorca always has for us. He speaks to us with a vocabulary which is directly related to the soil, to mother earth, to a simple rural society and to the cosmic universe.

It will be important to notice, on the other hand, that the objects of nature with which the poet was able to converse when he was a child and that continued to give him hints and suggestions in his adult and creative life will actually become a repertory of symbols underlying the texture of his poetry. The sun, the moon, the wind, the water, trees, grass, mountains, rivers, brooks, horses, bulls, cows, fish, birds, different kinds of plants and fruits, oleander, jazmin, pomegranate, lemons, oranges, rocks, pebbles, all of these enter into his poetry with powerful calls pointing to concrete experiences and coherent structures of meaning. In *Deep Song* (*Cante jondo*), one of Lorca's early books, the wind that blows through the olive trees carries all kinds of mysterious sounds, and is intermingled in a single experience with the green color of the groves, the neighing of the horses and the passionate shouts of people singing their songs of tormented love, out into the distant horizons of dark nights. In these poems, the sky is a continuation of the earth ("land of light/and sky of earth"), and black butterflies mix with white serpents to carry with them the dark-skinned girl of the gypsy song ("Siguiriya gitana"). The air vibrations at night and in the dawn are the same vibrations of the guitar strings, which, in turn, put in motion the foliage of the trees and the hair and skirts of the gypsy girls. The sound waves are reflected on the ondulations of the dry earth, the "ondulated desert." The long shades at dusk fuse with the burning grape vines and with the olive trees to form the labyrinthic maze within which man's destiny is being determined. Black and dreamy horses take men with inescapable fatality to a final labyrinth of crosses. Grief and dark premonitions permeate the landscape. Also, in his book of the *Gypsy Ballads* (*Romancero gitano*) the fate of man can be read in solidarity with the manifestations of nature. The death of a child and the drowning of a girl occur under the malignant influence of the moon light, at the moment when dawn is beginning to appear in the horizon. Men kill each other in a senseless fight ("Reyerta") in the midst of ill auguring signs in the sky (clouds, lightning and rain). The gypsy outlaw, who has to appear before the authorities ("El emplazado") can read his destiny in the hard and metal-like light of the nearby rocky hills. The black horses of the Civil Guard are, on the other hand, the carriers of bad omen for the city of the gypsies. Things and phenomena of nature acquire, thus, a symbolic significance in relation to human destiny and the realization of the self.

This compact solidarity of man and nature is expressed in a dramatic web of interrelations that gives rise to the texture of myth. If myth is fundamentally a fable, an archetypal story, in which the deep impulses of the subconscious and the representational world of primitive mentality are projected, then the whole spectacle of nature and man's actions and cognitions can be seen in the perspective of myth. We can observe three different levels in the presentation of myth in the poetry of Lorca. First, a spectacle of nature is seen in an anthropomorphic context of mutually interrelated movements. Second, a spectacle of nature is woven into an integrated story, in which man is an active participant. Third, a spectacle of nature is seen objectively as a mythical story, but it is one that has an avowed and direct relationship to the inner life of the poet. All of these levels of mythical representation come through the individual mind of the poet, since the poetic consciousness acts as the center of the interrelated movements, whether the mythical story is being played out in the external world, or whether there is an active participation between man and the universe. The mythical story conveys clarification to the content of the poetic consciousness.

It is of interest to notice that Lorca himself tried to shed light, on various occasions, on the process by which he came to grips with the problem of language and of the structuring of the poem. Although we can see changes of emphasis, in a very short span of five years, between a first stage in which he sees the faculty of the imagination as the instrument through which he gives expression to the content of his poetic vision, and a next stage in which he stresses the concepts of "evasion" and of "poetic logic," and finally one in which the mysterious impulses of the earth and the presence of death are his primary concern, we can, nevertheless, say that his various theories complement each other. On the one hand, he propounds for the clarity of vision. On the other hand, he incorporates in his formulations what could be called the darker aspects of the self and the earthy dimension of his inspiration. In one of his first lectures "The Poetic Image of Don Luis de Góngora," 1926 (pp. 62-83), these two traits are revealed in different proportions, with the first one, that of clarity of vision, prevailing over the second one. For Lorca, the important thing, in the case of Góngora, was his capacity to "tie down" his imagination, by imposing a measure of orderly limits in the material to be absorbed from the senses. Góngora, in effect, says Lorca, would not allow himself to be dragged by the dark forces of inertia or by the fleeting brilliancy in which so many unaware poets succumb. Lorca's vision of the hunting trip at night depicts this rigorous process of selection:

> The poet must press on to the hunt single-minded and serene; in virtual camouflage. He must stand firm in the presence of illusions and keep wary lookout for the quivering flesh of reality that accords with the shadowy map of the poem that he carries. At times, he will cry out loudly in the poem's solitude, to rout the evil spirits—facile ones who would betray us to popular adulation without order or beauty or esthetic understanding.[2]

The resulting landscape will be one of order and clarity: "An ordered countryside, in which poetry itself sets the limits to its own feverish rapture." This formulation by Lorca is a far cry from the chaotic landscape alluded to by André Breton in his first declaration of surrealist doctrine.[3] In another of his lectures, the one on "Imagination, Inspiration and Evasion" (pp. 85-91), Lorca defines the notions of "poetic truth," "poetic emotion," "poetic logic" and "poetic fact," and asserts that they are *sui generis,* that is, of an entirely different nature from the products of rational thinking. According to Lorca, the poetic fact is by definition a non-rational phenomenon, although it implies a coherent and significant design. Also, the notion of poetic logic does not exclude in any way the notion of complete freedom of the inspiration and of the absence of limits. In a letter Lorca addressed to his friend Sebastian Gasch in 1928, he says of the two new poems he is sending to him: "They reflect my new spiritualized manner, they contain a pure and bare emotion, completely devoid of all logical control, although ¡Beware! ¡Beware!, with a tremendous amount of poetic logic. Indeed, they have nothing to do with surrealism, ¡Beware!, the clearest consciousness illuminates them" (p. 1654). Lorca finds, thus, that even at the moments of his greatest freedom and inspiration he is still guided by norms in his process of creation.

This personal will of the poet to an ordered created structure for the poem takes into account, on the other hand, the absorption into his poetry of the darker forces of nature and of his own subconscious. Lorca's poetry is characterized precisely by the presence of the mysterious in man and nature. In other of his theoretical pronouncements, he actually emphasizes these other aspects of the poetic process. In his lecture on "Childhood Cradle Songs", 1928 (pp. 91-108), for instance, he stresses how important it is for the poet to submerge himself into the deep river beds of traditional popular poetry. The poet's inspiration cannot but be enriched by his submersion. Nevertheless, even here, Lorca refers to that "abstract quality" which is projected in some of the landscapes that are suggested by these popular songs. This abstract dimension allows the mind of the child to enter into distant mysterious spaces. Also, in his two lectures on the *Cante jondo*, the first one of the year 1922 and the second one of the year 1931 (pp. 39-61), the poet emphasizes the primitive quality of the inspiration in this kind of art, which fuses both the musical and the poetic. The primitive impulses of the *Cante* are manifested in thoughts of life and death and are charged with deep emotional content. Once more, nevertheless, the poet points to what consistutes the organizing and stylizing features in the poetry of the *Deep Song* couplets: "There is nothing, absolutely nothing in the whole of Spain, similar to it in the manner of stylization, or in the projected atmosphere, or in the precision of the emotional content" (p. 45). Finally, in his lecture on the "Theory and Play of the *Duende*" (pp. 109-121), Lorca thinks that the great moments of authentic and original poetic creation are related to the presence of the forces of the earth and to the powerful pulsations of one's own blood. For Lorca, the *Duende* (in its Andalusian meaning of creative originality) is "a power rather than an acting," and one that leads to a real confrontation with it in the moments of its appearance. The *Duende* excludes all exercise in thinking ("es un luchar y no un pensar"). It burns the blood and makes the poetic form explode, bringing with it the miraculous presence of newly created sensations, which prompt a religious enthusiasm. The *Duende* is bound to the roots of the earth, it is the spirit of the earth, and expresses itself in black sounds and black strokes of the brush: "These black sounds constitute the mystery, the roots that are nailed down to the very mud and which all of us recognize, even if we don't know much about it, but from which comes all that is essential in art." With the appearance of the *Duende* there is the persistent look of death, lying in ambush behind us. It is this condition of the *Duende* what gives the magic quality to the poem. Lorca points, at the same time, that it is on the arena of the bullfight, where the *Duende* reveals itself with overwhelming features, since it is here where it has to fight, on the one side with the abyss of death, and on the other with geometry. It is geometry and measure, says Lorca "that which constitutes the fundamental basis of the bullfight" (p. 119). Thus, once again, Lorca introduces the notion of order, when dealing with the presence of the darker impulses of poetic creation. The poet himself has given us clues for the interpretation of his poetry. The dark impulses coexist with the will to the clarity of vision. Myth and the mythification of nature will become one of the ordering paths in Lorca's poetic inspiration.

We shall now give concrete examples of the three levels of mythical patterns that appear in the poetry of Lorca. At the first level, the poem entitled "Fable" ("Fábula"), of his book *Canciones* (1921-1924), presents the well known mythological figures of the Cyclops and the Unicorns in deadly confrontation with one another, in a hurried stampeeding against the cliffs of the water's edge. There is no doubt that the cyclops, with their green eyes, are the projected figures of the green waves of sea water, while the unicorns appear as the embodiment of the reflections of light over the water:

> Unicornios y cíclopes.
>
> Una pupila
> y una potencia.
> ¿Quién duda de la eficacia
> terrible de esos cuernos?
> ¡Oculta tus blancos,
> Naturaleza!   (p. 365)

The last words of the poem are a warning to Nature by the poet, in view of the efficacious power of the unicorns: "Nature, Hide your targets." The dramatic confrontation of the two sets of physical phenomena in the world of nature, that is, light and waves, which becomes a struggle of unicorns and cyclops at the level of myth, can certainly be symbolically referred to the creative forces of the artist. The unicorns, with their objective referent to light, point to the conscious and, therefore, ordering aspect of artistic creation. On the other hand, the bare forces of the cyclops, with their referent to the unrushing waves of the sea, represent the tumultous and chaotic forces of the subconscious and of poetic inspiration. In the end, the sea waves are hit by the horns of light.

The ballad "Preciosa and the Wind" ("Preciosa y el aire") exemplifies the second level of mythification of nature, that in which man is an active participant. The anthropomorphizing impulses start in the mind of the gypsy girl, who gives to a sudden gush of wind the attributes of an agressive lover ("viento hombrón"). The latter, in turn, threatens her with the loss of her virginity. The wind unleashes a real storm, which is then accompanied by lightning and rain and continues the persecution of the girl with its hot sword ("espada caliente") and its shining tongues. The frightened girl runs full of terror and takes refuge in a nearby house, while the masculine wind keeps on biting at the roof of the house. It is clear that in this story, the cosmic forces of the wind and storm act at the level of human configurations establishing, thereby, an interrupted continuum between man and nature. This makes possible the creation of a plot of lascivious pursuing the panicky fleeing. Such structure of meaning is magically enhanced by the presence of powerful images of light and fire, and by the cosmic orchestration of sounds, colors and the phenomena of temperature. The *Duende* makes here its appearance radiating its power into the projection of a well constructed and primitive story.

At the third level of mythical configuration, we find the enactment of a mythical story which is played out in a spectacle of nature, and which has a direct relationship to the inner life of the poet. Here, myth is an objectivization of subjective and unconscious states of mind, with a strong emotional content. Lorca builds up a trajectory of mythical representation that is related to human destiny, but also to his career as an artist, and to the broader context of the realization of the self. The poem "Adam" of his early book *Primeras canciones,* 1922, reveals the structure of a mythical plot concerning the birth of a new son out of the cosmic parents, the sun as the father and the moon as the mother of the newly-born day. The sun father, feverishly dreams of the new child that rushingly gallops over the pulsating beat of his two cheeks. This happens after the birth has taken place in a bloody spectacle ("Arbol de sangre moja la mañana"), and the bewailing mother, with no blood left in her veins, is forced to flee in emaciating paleness ("y un gráfico de hueso en la ventana"). Nevertheless, the poet contemplates this renewed story of the birth of the day and the presence of the energizing forces of nature, with a feeling of utter helplessness and frustration. He sees himself, in effect, as another "Adam," who only will be able to father a son that will burn out into nothingness, since he lacks the energizing power of the cosmic sun. The last tercet of the sonnet establishes the connection between the archetypal cosmic spectacle and the degraded personal story of a birth which is doomed to failure:

> Pero otro Adán oscuro está soñando
> neutra luna de piedra sin semilla
> donde el niño de luz se irá quemando. (p. 353)

The obscure Adam (the poet) can only dream of images of sterility ("a sexless stone moon without any seed"), which no doubt have to do with the feeling of lack of artistic potency.

The cosmic plot of the archetypal family and the birth of the day will soon expand in Lorca's poetry into a wide context of symbolization. In fact, the end of the day will constitute the continuation of the myth, since the red colorations of the sky at the moment of the sunset, is seen as another bloody spectacle that marks the death of the powerful mythical figure. The death of the sun makes possible, in turn, the appearance of the moon, whose full dominance in the horizon has a portentous influence on the life of man. If the sun implies vitality and the full realization of the self, the moon acts as an evil omen on man's trajectory. The two symbols are, thus, interrelated to one another, not only by their mutual position in the mythical story (man, wife and son), but also by the fact that their movements are determined by astronomical laws, including the succession of day and night. Their location in the sky, particularly at the moment of dawn and dusk and during the night, and also their coloration and shape, or even their full presence or absence, will reflect variations in their mythical representation, and, ultimately, in their manner of signification. The poetic structure will, thus, present definable signals, which will guide us in the process of decodifying its own meaning. The mythical story allows for the fusion of the obscure with the clear, of the shapeless with the schematic, of the undefinable with that which is plastically projected in figures, colors, and contrasts of light and darkness, all this within the texture of cosmic events.

It is to be noted, on the other hand, that the original plot of the birth and death of the day, marked by the appearance and disappearance of the sun and the counterpart movement of the disappearance and then the appearance of the moon in the horizon, is intertwined in the poetry of Lorca with the presence of the bull and the cow, in correlation with the figures of the cosmic father and mother. In Egyptian mythology, the solar god Osiris, the father, is the bull Apis, and the moon goddess Isis, the mother, is the cow. Out of the union of the two parents the child Horus is born. In fact, we can infer that Lorca found his correlation of the cosmic father, mother and son, from some knowledge of Egyptian mythology.[4] On the other hand, the sunset will constitute for Lorca the enactment of the killing of the mythical figure, an event which will be associated with the killing of the bull on the arena of the bullfight. Moreover, the killing of the bull, that is, the sunset, will also be associated in Lorca with the myth of Saint John the Baptist, as it appears in Mallarmé's poem *Hérodiade.* The last part of Mallarmé's poem is entitled, in effect, "Canticle of Saint John" ("Cantique de Saint Jean"), and has as its theme the decapitation of Saint John, which, in the poem, is also the beheading of the sun, although in reference to the summer's solstice, rather than to the sunset. This cosmic event coincides with the day of Saint John the Baptist, which takes place on the twenty fourth of June.[5] All these correlations appear in Lorca's prose poem "The Beheading of the Baptist" ("Degollación del Bautista, pp. 27-29), which was written around 1928, the same year in which he gave his lecture on "Imagination, Inspiration and Evasion." The poem presents masses of people, who are lined up as observers of a great spectacle, in which the actual participants in the confrontation are divided in two teams, the Reds and the Blacks, hence the reference to a large stadium, rather than specifically to the arena of the bullfight. The two colors imply, nevertheless, an allusion to the sun and shade areas in the disposition of the seats around the arena of the bullfight or of the stadium, according to which the various locations are termed "Sol y Sombra" or "Blanco y Negro," and in our poem "Rojos y Negros." The two colors appear here, nevertheless, as the actual name of the confronting teams. The division in Reds and Blacks alludes, on the other hand, to the colorations of red in the horizon and the approaching darkness of late afternoon. The spectacle of the "Degollación del Bautista" enacts, thus, the scene of the decapitation of Saint John, with implications of the killing of the bull in the sky and on the arena, in unison with the setting of the sun. The last part of the poem refers to the actual moment of the beheading of the mythical figure, in the midst of shouting crowds:

> El griterío del Estadium hizo que las vacas mugieran en todos los establos de Palestina. La cabeza del luchador celeste estaba en medio de la arena. Las jovencitas se teñían las mejillas de rojo y los jóvenes pintaban sus corbatas en el cañón estremecido de la yugular desgarrada.

La cabeza de Bautista:	¡Luz!
Los rojos:	Filo
La cabeza de Bautista:	¡Luz! ¡Luz!
Los rojos:	Filo filo
La cabeza de Bautista:	Luz luz luz
Los rojos:	Filo filo filo filo. (p. 28)

In addition to the figures of the bull and the cow, there is also in the poetry of Lorca, the figure of the horse, as one of the essential components of the mythical plot. The horse is of paramount importance in Andalusian culture and plays a constant role in the life of the gypsies. In the *Romancero gitano*, the horse allows man to move from one place to another and eventually leads him to meet his own destiny of death. In the context of the cosmic story, in Lorca's vision, the horse is identified with the rounded horizon, the celestial abode, which becomes the rump of the horse, and which keeps moving in order to let the protagonists appear in the sky and have their encounters. The image of the horizon as the rump of a shiny colt occurs in the ballad "Prendimiento de Antoñito el Camborio" (p. 445), at the moment when Antoñito is taken to prison to be later executed:

> Y a las nueve de la noche
> le cierran el calabozo,
> mientras el cielo reluce
> como la grupa de un pobro.

Also, in the ballad "Martirio de Santa Olalla" (p. 458), the dark night appears as a long tailed horse that runs and jumps among the streets of Mérida, while Roman soldiers await sleepingly the hour of the execution of Saint Eulalia:

> Por la calle brinca y corre
> caballo de larga cola,
> mientras juegan o dormitan
> viejos soldados de Roma.

We should remember now that in the poem "Adam," the newly born creature appears galloping along a horse: "Adán sueña en la fiebre de la arcilla/un niño que se acerca galopando/por el doble latir de su mejilla" (p. 353). The horse is, thus, the dynamic impulse that sets in motion the other figures of the mythical story. Man's destiny is tied up to the inevitability of their movements and their encounters. As the sun, the primeval Adam, inexorably moves toward its own beheading, so is man's destiny, essentially a tragic one. The moon, in turn, radiates its own evil influence at night, from which there is no escaping. Man is a participant in this mythical story, together with the other figures that move on their own trajectory in the cosmic universe. The mythical plot helps to clarify man's destiny, and to give the mysterious and dark impulses of life a symbolic representation in an ordered pattern.

Although Lorca absorbed early into his poetry some of the components of his mythic vision, it is in the years 1927-1928, the period of composition of his prose poems, when he seems to have fully developed the mythic plot into a tight structure of mutual interrelations. This can be seen in the "Beheading of the Baptist," but also in some of his other prose poems. In his letter to Sebastián Gasch, he alludes to the fact that he is sending him the two "degollaciones," out of three that he intends to write. We might surmise that the "Degollación del Bautista" was one of them. A second one could very well be the "Degollación de los inocentes" (pp. 29-30), whose very title alludes to the act of beheading. In this prose poem, the end of the massacre of the innocent children takes place at the end of the day, when blood is being splashed on all clocks at six in the afternoon:

> A las seis de la tarde ya no quedaban más que seis niños por degollar. Los relojes de arena seguían sangrando, pero ya estaban secas todas las heridas.

In another prose poem, "Santa Lucía y San Lázaro" (pp. 13-19), there appear images of physical violence, since Saint Lucia's martyrdom consisted of the gouging of her eyes. The other protagonist, Saint Lazarus, suffered death, was buried and then miraculously resurrected, according to the biblical story. The narrator in the poem travels to a town where he takes lodge and board at midnight in Saint Lucía's Inn (Posada de Santa Lucía). The next day, he goes around watching all activities, and in the afternoon he is able to observe that the show-cases in the stores are full of optical lens and prisms, and that monstrous eyes ("ojos terribles") are hanging in the horizon out of their pupils. There is here, no doubt, a reference to Saint Lucia's eyes, but also to the particular kind of light that now filters in the atmosphere. The moment finally approaches for the red coloration in the sky, which announces the beheading of the Baptist:

> Gafas y vidrios ahumados buscaban la inmensa mano cortada de la guantería, poema en el aire, que suena, sangra y borbotea como la cabeza del Bautista (p. 15).

Concurrently, religious services are being conducted in the cathedral in honor of Saint Lucia. It is the moment in which horror prevails, on account of the impending blood-spout outside:

> El mundo de la hierba se oponía al mundo del mineral. La uña, contra el corazón. Dios de contorno, transparencia y superficie. Con el miedo al latido y el horror al chorro de sangre, se pedía la tranquilidad de las ágatas y la desnudez sin sombra de la medusa (p. 16).

In the second part of the poem, the narrator walks toward the railroad station at night, which happens to be Saint Lazarus Railroad Station. On the way to his destination, he can still see Saint Lucia's eyes over the sea, by the side of the still bleeding bust: "Ojos de Santa Lucía en el mar, en la esfera del reloj, a los lados del yunque, en el gran tronco recién cortado." At two o'clock in the morning, he can see that another traveler is approaching with deathly eyes and dressed in a white suit. His intense paleness has the color of plaster and eggs: "Su mano derecha era de duro yeso y llevaba colgado del brazo un cesto de mimbre lleno de huevos de gallina." In addition, this is the night when Spain celebrates the great festivity (an apparent allusion to Saint John's night). Finally, a voice is heard calling Lázarus, and the strange traveler fades away among the last lights. By the imagery of the poem and the narrative thread, it seems clear that the situation of the story and its religious protagonists have to do with the phenomena of light in the horizon, particularly in the late afternoon and early dawn. The esoteric texture of the poem could very well correspond to what Lorca called the "poetic fact" in his lectures "Imagination, Inspiration and Evasion." The goughing of Saint Lucia's eyes is related to the beheading of the sun, through the images of blood. On the other hand, the appearance of the deathly Saint Lazarus, with his faint and whitish light, would be a forerunner of the resurrected sun.

It is with *Poet in New York,* nevertheless, that the full implications of the myth are revealed for Lorca's tragic vision, in the perspective of his own personal life. Lorca's trip to New York in the summer of 1929 brings him, in effect, to the alien atmosphere of a technologically advanced city culture, that is basically deprived of a direct communication with nature. In fact, there is no rural landscape in New York and whatever is left of nature is diminished by the presence of the tall skyscrapers along the narrow streets and the absence of daylight in the dark subway tunnels. Moreover, with the approach of Fall and Winter, with their cloudy skies, the sun and the moon rarely appear in the horizon. Also, the trees are without leaves and snow and slush cover the ground. Within this landscape, man's life is not fully integrated with the pulsations of nature, and so, his destiny is marked by the signs of sterility. The mythical figures have been mutilated and appear totally degraded. In the poem "Cow" ("Vaca," p. 503), for instance, one of the earliest of the collection, the feminine figure has been mortally wounded at dawn ("se tendió la vaca herida"), and its body has been cut into pieces, with its four hooves left trembling in the air ("Cuatro pezuñas tiemblan en el aire"). In a later poem, "Dawn" ("La aurora," p. 497), the dawn in New York collapses over its four pillars of mud, while a storm of black doves splash from the rotten waters. The early risers who come out of their homes know that they will drown in the mud of figures and norms. Others walk along, half asleep, as if coming from a bloody shipwreck. Also, in the poem "The Birth of Christ" ("Nacimiento de Cristo," p. 496), the bull can only dream of a bull full of holes and water, and the child weeps with the number three on his forehead. The birth of the Christ child is thus frustrated by the ominous signs of rain in the sky. On the other hand, the symbol of the dead child, or of the utterly fragile creature, who will die while being born, is one of the prevailing ones in the poems of *Poet in New York*. A dying child is bemoaned by the barking dogs in the poem "Unsleeping City" ("Ciudad sin sueño"): "y el niño que enterraron esta mañana lloraba tanto/que hubo necesidad de llamar a los perros para que callase" (p. 493). Similarly, the moon appears in the horizon without its fertilizing attributes, as if it were a stone without seeds, or is identified with the skull of a horse, as in the poem "Ruin" ("Ruina"): "Pronto se vio que la luna/era una calavera de caballo/y el aire una manzana oscura" (p. 511).

This degradation of the mythical figures in *Poet in New York* is, no doubt, a symbolic projection of the poet's lack of emotional and artistic self realization. Love here never reaches fulfillment, or it is strangled in the very initial process of its being manifested. On the other hand, the poet has to wrestle with the chaotic impulses of his creative power. Hence, the accumulation of negative signs and the ominous presence of the dead child. In the poem "Nocturne of the Void" ("Nocturno del hueco"), the powerful mythical figure has been beheaded at dawn over the empty arena: "En la gran plaza desierta/mugía la cabeza recién cortada." This event coincides with a love that has withered away and only offers empty gloves and hollow dresses. The girating voids are projected from the inner soul of the poet into the sky and on the face of the wounded moon:

Ruedan los huecos puros, por mí, por ti, en el alba

conservando las huellas de las ramas de sangre
y algún perfil de yeso tranquilo que dibuja
instantáneo dolor de luna apuntillada. (p. 508)

In the second part of the "Nocturne of the Void" (p. 507), the poet finds himself in complete solitude, inside empty spaces and only with the company of the very white void of a horse, which has ashes in its mane. The horizon at dawn has thus been emptied of the mythical presence of the horse, and does not even show any imprints of blood:

Yo.
Con el hueco blanquísimo de un caballo.
Rodeado de espectadores que tienen hormigas en las palabras.

En el circo del frío sin perfil mutilado.
Por los capiteles rotos de la mejillas desangradas. (p. 509)

The poet's life has been anchored, with no feeling of movement: "Ecuestre por mi vida definitivamente anclada."

The poem "Cricifixion" (p. 532) fuses the cosmic impact of a dark and rainy day with the religious symbols of the crucifixion of Christ. The moon appears at dawn on the very white curve of a horse, although the child is already dead at the very moment of the circumcision. The weeping that can be heard coming from the south is due to the fact that the moon has been burning the phallus of horses in candle fire. A skull appears in the sky and is contemplated through the window by the three Holy Virgins. The galaxies are rusty and have been nailed down with thorns. Rain begins to fall drenching hearts and streets. At this point, the pharisees accurse the moon for the milk and birdshots she is sending down to earth. In the afternoon, the sun has not yet appeared in the horizon, although the moment of redemption will be revealed, as soon as the moon has bathed with water drops the blistering horse-flesh. When night time comes, the pharisees withdraw to their houses in the midst of bloody taints in the sky. They accurse the moon for not letting them sleep. The poem ends with a parodic biblical allusion:

Fue entonces
y la tierra despertó arrojando temblorosos ríos de polilla.

Man's destiny has, thus, lost all meaning in this vision of New York, where the mythical figures have been emasculated and degraded. There is no hope of salvation for man when deprived of a real participation with nature and the cosmic universe.

It is significant that after his New York experience, Lorca's poetic vision reaches the full strength of man's participation in the mythical plot. Man's destiny is indeed a tragic one, but his life is enhanced and made meaningful by his solidarity with the forces of nature. In *Blood Wedding* (1933), the passionate lovers, Leonardo and the Bride, flee from the scene of the wedding following the dictates of their most inner and dark impulses. In the end, the killing of the lover and the bridegroom takes place in the open spaces at night, under the ominous influence of the red moon light. In *Lament for Ignacio Sánchez Mejías* (1935), the death of the bullfighter occurs when he is facing the real bull on the arena, and at the moment when the other bull in the sky is close to its own beheading. The blood of the bullfighter's sacrifice is subsequently drunk by the thirsty ancient cow ("vaca del Viejo Mundo"), the cow of the Old World, the mythical figure which now appears in the sky with its unequivocal signs of an evil omen. The bullfighter's strength and vitality have been broken down by fate, but his life has been made significant by the full presence of the mythical figures. The bullfighter's blood drenches the arena and filters through the earth in a ritual sacrifice that fulfills the solidarity of man and cosmos. Lorca saw in nature man's way to self fulfillment, but also the inevitability of his own tragic destiny.

Gustavo Correa
Yale University

NOTES

[1] Federico García Lorca, *Obras completas* (fourteenth edition, Madrid: Aguilar, 1968), p. 1974. All of our quotations and translations are from this edition.

[2] *Obras completas*, p. 74. Here the translation is by Ben Helitt, *Poet in New York* (New York, 1955), p. 176.

[3] "On traverse, avec un tressaillement, ce que les occultistes appellent des *paysages dangereux*. Je suscite sur mes pas des monstres qui gettent, ils ne sont pas encore trop malintentionnés a mon égard et je ne suis pas perdu, puisque je les crains. Voici 'les éléphants à tête de femme et les lions volants' que, Soupault et moi, nous tremblâmes naguère de rencontrer, voici le 'poisson soluble,' qui m'effraye bien encore un peu. *Poisson soluble*, n'est-ce pas moi le poisson soluble, je suis né sous le signe des Poissons et l'homme est soluble dans sa pensée! La faune et la flore du surréalisme sont inavouables," in André Breton, *Les manifestes du surréalisme* (Paris, 1946), p. 66.

[4] See my article "El simbolismo del sol en la poesía de Federico García Lorca," *NRFH*, XIV (1960), pp. 110-119.

[5] See Wallace Fowlie, *Mallarmé* (Chicago, 1953), p. 140.

THE CHANGING VIEW OF NATURE IN FEDERICO GARCÍA LORCA

In his introduction to García Lorca's *Obras Completas,* Jorge Guillén, poet of the Generation of 1927 and a personal friend, has written words which reveal and define the character of the poet from Granada and the essence of his literary production:

> Federico García Lorca fue una criatura extraordinaria. "Criatura" significa esta vez más que "hombre." Porque Federico nos ponía en contacto con la creación...[1]

Federico García Lorca: a creature in the midst of creation, part of creation, totally immersed in and identified with creation. In his own words:

> Quiero llorar diciendo mi nombre,
> rosa, niño y abeto a la orilla de este lago,
> para decir mi verdad de hombre de sangre
> matando en mí la burla y la suggestión del vocablo.[2]

This feeling of oneness and total immersion in the universe, especially nature, may be partially due to his up-bringing in the countryside. Lorca's biographers describe the child Federico as almost talking and communicating with animals and plants. It may also be due to his being an Andalusian who, according to Ortega y Gasset, has "a vegetal sense of existence."[3]

But Federico García Lorca is not a poet of nature as we usually understand the term. Nature in his works is not a beautiful motif or a background for man's actions. Both man and nature are a real *presence,* equally alive and intertwined in the universe, influencing each other, struggling against each other or complementing each other in a blind fulfillment of their cosmic destiny. Throughout his work, in poetry as well as in theater, basic values of freedom, individualism, love, and creativity are viewed as fruits of man's ability to live in harmony with nature. Conversely, a break with nature is the cause of man's frustration and dehumanization. The poet's role is to be there, with his finger on the pulse of all creation, probing the mystery and the drama of the universe:

> porque yo no soy un hombre, ni un poeta, ni una hoja, ¡pero sí un pulso herido que sonda las cosas del otro lado.[4]

As both the poet and his work develop and mature in years, the view of nature and its relationship to man change significantly. This change is reflected in thematic treatment and in poetic language. Years ago, my first study of Lorca's poetry, based almost exclusively on stylistic analysis, revealed the existence of three well defined periods, characterized by predominance of emblems, metaphors, and symbols, as vehicles of concretizing abstraction, visual contemplation, and intuitive insight respectively.[5] Now, many years later, an interesting observation may explain to some degree the cause of these changes in the poetic language of García Lorca. This observation concerns *the changing point of view,* and I shall attempt to apply it to Lorca's treatment of nature.

The Spanish writer and dramatist of the generation preceeding Lorca's, Ramón del Valle-Inclán, defined the point of view an author may take as follows:

> ...creo hay tres modos de ver el mundo, artística o estéticamente: de rodillas, en pie o levantado en el aire.[6]

Valle-Inclán goes on to explain that the view on one's knees is how Homer saw his heroes; standing or face-to-face is how Shakespeare saw his; and from the air, how Cervantes, Quevedo or Goya saw theirs. The first is the case of the author's admiring attitude toward the object described; the second point of view places him face-to-face with the object and on equal footing; the third is an impassive view of an un-involved spectator.

As we read Lorca's first book of poems, *Libro de poemas,* we realize at once that the young poet, barely twenty years old, faces the world with awe and reverence. Whatever he sees, he admires. Everything he admires, he so does because he views it as part of the total creation. Nature, its most visible component, becomes the central point, the common denominator to which all creatures are reduced or likened. This attitude prevails in most poems. Whether he speaks of the tragedy of a sterile woman ("Elegía") or the love-frustration of a princess ("Elegía a Doña Juana la Loca"), he does so *on his knees*. The reference to nature is constant. Doña Juana is a "red carnation in a deep and desolate valley;" she is a dove; her song is that of a lark; her passion reflects the sky of Spain; on her death, the landscape of Granada becomes an immense cathedral:

> Granada era tu lecho de muerte, Doña Juana; los cipreses, tus cirios; la sierra, tu retablo.

A similar, perhaps even more intense admiration is awarded the sterile woman whose death signals her total transformation and incorporation into the universe:

> Tu cuerpo irá a la tumba intacto de emociones.
> Sobre la oscura tierra brotará una alborada.
> De tus ojos saldrán dos claveles sangrientos,
> y de tus senos, rosas como la nieve blancas.
> Pero tu gran tristeza se irá con las estrellas,
> como otra estrella digna de herirlas y eclipsarlas.[7]

Such Homeric admiration *on his knees* is not limited, however, to Lorca's human characters. We observe the same attitude, at times even more pronounced, when the poet speaks of a cicada or a lizard, a tree, a star, or the wind. They all form part of the universe he admires. They all become central characters and participate in the glory and in the tragedy of life and death. Just as in the case of the sterile woman, the "enchanted" cicada dies and is transfigured into heavenly sound and light:

> Mas tú, cigarra encantada,
> derramando son, te mueres
> y quedas transfigurada
> en sonido y luz celeste.

And further down:

>   ...el sol le lleva tu alma
>   para hacerla luz.[8]

Even in this early poetry, one can find all the essential elements of Lorca's future concern for cosmic harmony, disrupted by man, his ideas and his unnatural laws. The thought of Marcus Aurelius, the faith of Socrates, or the heart of Juan de Dios are poor when compared to the song of cicada, the flow of a river or the beauty of a rose.[9] And the poet himself turns toward nature, communicates with it and learns about life from it:

> Yo, como el barbudo mago de los cuentos,
> sabía el lenguaje de flores y piedras.
>
> Aprendí secretos de melancolía,
> dichos por cipreses, ortigas y yedras;
> supe del ensueño por boca de nardo,
> canté con los lirios canciones serenas.[10]

The strong, sometimes excessive, reliance on nature and its power changes gradually the point of view of the poet. In his later work, from the *Poema del Cante Jondo* and through the *Romancero gitano,* García Lorca abandons his admiring attitude and adopts a more analytical and detached posture of an impassive observer *from the air.* The exciting mystery of a marvelous universe is replaced by an intuitive view of a world dominated by dark forces which fatalistically determine human destiny. Nature, now almost hostile to man, is viewed increasingly by the poet as a living and vibrating presence: silence is ondulating, water carries "a fatuous flame of screams,"[11] the grey air curls, wind vibrates or cries, reeds and shadows tremble, streets quiver. There is a menacing feeling of ever-present violent death and the cosmic forces intervene in man's life and exert a mysterious influence on him. Moon casts its spell on life as it appears in a forge to take away a child ("Romance de la luna, luna"); water has a magnetic influence on a gypsy girl ("Romance sonámbulo"); wind becomes a sensuous satyr who pursues a girl trying to seduce her ("Preciosa y el aire").

The poet, now an emotionally detached observer, impassively views the drama that unfolds on the cosmic stage, unable to admire neither nature, hostile and vengeful, nor man, who becomes a puppet in the hands of fate. This is the intermediate period of Lorca's work; his new point of view is reflected in his series of farces and in his poetry. A common characteristic is an almost total absence of emotion. It is highly significant that Lorca's dramatic production of this period, especially *Amor de Don Perlimplín* and *La zapatera prodigiosa*, borders on tragedy but dissolves in a farce. Equally revealing is his emotionless treatment of gypsies in the *Romancero gitano*, where tragic death is expressed in cold historic terms of:

> Señores guardias civiles,
> aquí pasó lo de siempre;
> han muerto cuatro romanos
> y cinco cartagineses.[12]

The reason seems clear: García Lorca views his characters *from the air*, impassively. He considers them puppets and refuses to identify himself humanly with their plight.

Nature fares no better during this period. The *Romancero gitano* is curiously void of extended passages devoted to nature. With one minor exception ("San Gabriel"), no poem of this book shows nature in its beauty. Passing references to nature highlight a dramatic and unfriendly image: cold and frosty nights, stormy winds, cloudy skies, "bitter-green" air. Moreover, nature seems bent on displaying its hostility:

> el agua se pone fría
> para que nadie la toque[13]

and

> con el aire se batían
> las espadas de los lirios.[14]

and

> ...las estrellas clavan
> rejones al agua gris[15]

and

> ...el cielo daba portazos
> al brusco rumor del bosque.[16]

Then, in 1929, a new dimension and a new point of view open up in the work of García Lorca. The poet's trip to New York places him *face-to-face* with reality. In the impending depression life of New York, García Lorca discovers that man's and nature's struggle for survival is not a poetic theme, but a harsh and tragic fact filled with suffering and anguish. The gigantic conflict is staged neither by Homeric heroes nor by mysterious cosmic forces, but rather by the unchallenged advance of modern technology which ruthlessly tramples men and nature alike.

To fully understand Lorca's change of point of view, we may recall Ortega y Gasset's example of different attitudes people adopt when viewing the agony of a dying man[17]: an artist observes the scene as a picture in which the setting (room, lights and shadows, facial expressions, etc.) provides him with a creative stimulus; a physician views the situation with a professional eye; a newspaper reporter readies a story with just enough emotional sprinklings to attract readers' attention; only the dying man's wife is humanly involved and shares the anxiety and suffering of her husband.

This last attitude defines García Lorca's new point of view. He discovers at last a true *human* dimension of the on-going conflict which leaves him no room for admiration *on his knees* nor allows him to remain an impassive observer *from the air*, but forces him to view reality *face-to-face*. For the first time, Federico García Lorca identifies himself with the victim of the conflict, be it the oppressed man or the mutilated nature. Indeed this identification reveals to him that he himself, as part of creation, is being threatened with destruction and moves him to voice his protest against the existing situation:

> entre las formas que van hacia la sierpe
> y las formas que buscan el cristal,
> dejaré crecer mis cabellos.[18]

Poems of *Poeta en Nueva York* are filled with images of men, women, and children ravished by opression, materialism, degradation, and total dehumanization. But it is nature that draws his deepest sympathy. No longer a powerful cosmic force, nature is the most obvious victim of modern technology. A tree "in a cage of cement," a "butterfly drowned in an inkwell," a "dove cast into sewers," a "cat flattened to sheet-metal," "trains of manacled roses, chained by the drummers of perfume," are only a few examples of the immense tragedy affecting nature; they are at the same time individual symbols of destruction summed up in one total symbolic description of nature crushed by technology:

> Hay un mundo de ríos quebrados y distancias inasibles en la patita de ese gato quebrada por el automóvil.[19]

The complete involvement, sympathy, and militant defense of nature go one step further as García Lorca not only denounces the conspiracy against nature but actually offers himself to be sacrificed as a propitiatory victim for the redemption of the agonizing creation:

> No, no; yo denuncio,
> yo denuncio la conjura
> de estas desiertas oficinas
> que no radian las agonías,
> que borran los programas de la selva,
> y me ofrezco a ser comido por las vacas estrujadas
> cuando sus gritos llenan el valle
> donde el Hudson se emborracha con aceite.[20]

The degree of personal involvement in a cause marks an important change in García Lorca's attitude. The poet, heretofore unconcerned with political, social, or ideological issues (for him the gypsy was never of a real concern), finds himself committed to an active struggle against all evils of modern civilization. His symbolic "Cry to Rome (From the Chrysler Building Tower)" is a powerful condemnation of a world where peace, love, and social justice have become all but forgotten virtues. His militancy against immorality, materialism, and opression, embodied in the image of the cruel and ruthless financial center of Wall Street where the banker computes "the merciless silence of money" leads him to prophesy its total destruction and ultimate victory of nature:

> Que ya las cobras silbarán por los últimos pisos,
> que ya las ortigas estremecerán patios y terrazas,
> que ya la Bolsa será una pirámide de musgo,
> que ya vendrán lianas después de los fusiles
> y muy pronto, muy pronto, muy pronto.
> ¡Ay, Wall Street! [21]

This change of point of view, which makes the poet face reality and takes sides in the defense of nature against modern technological civilization, has a lasting effect on future life and work of Federico García Lorca. When he returns to Spain in 1930, he has already learned to view reality *face-to-face*. He no longer recreates poetic figures such as gypsies, who have little *real* significance in Spanish life, but turns instead to common people and their problems. His work becomes increasingly dramatic and carries a strong social message. Fully conscious of this change, García Lorca explains his new point of view in a 1936 interview, shortly before his tragic death:

> In this dramatic moment of the world, the artist must cry and laugh with his people. One must set aside the bouquet of lillies and enter into mud up to the waist in order to help those who search for lillies. Personally, I have a true yearning to communicate with others. That's why I called at the doors of theatre and now devote all my sensibility to it.[22]

And in another, earlier interview (1935) he also defines his work as a form of protest against a world full of injustice and misery.[23] One cannot but wonder whether it wasn't this final change of point of view that put Federico García Lorca *face-to-face* with his own ultimate reality: death before a firing squad.

Michael J. Flys
Arizona State University

NOTES

[1] Guillén, Jorge. Prólogo a FGL. *Obras completas,* Vol. I, 19ed., Aguilar, Madrid, 1974, p. XV.

[2] "Poema doble del lago Edén," *Poeta en Nueva York.*

[3] in *Teoría de Andalucía, Obras completas,* Vol. VI, *Revista de Occidente,* 6ed., Madrid, 1966, pp. 111-120.

[4] "Poema doble del lago Edén," *Poeta en Nueva York.*

[5] *El lenguaje poético de Federico García Lorca,* Ed. Gredos, Madrid, 1955.

[6] Martínez Sierra, Gregorio. "Hablando con Valle-Inclán. De él y su obra," *ABC* (Madrid), December 7, 1928, p. 1.

[7] "Elegía"

[8] "Cigarra"

[9] "Preguntas," *Libro de poemas.*

[10] "Invocación al Laurel"

[11] "Baladilla de los tres ríos," *Poema del Cante Jondo.*

[12] "Reyerta"

[13] "San Miguel"

[14] "Casada infiel"

[15] "Muerte de Antoñito el Camborio"

[16] "Muerto de amor"

[17] in *La deshumanización del arte, Obras completas*, Vol. III.

[18] "Vuelta de paseo"

[19] "New York. Oficina y denuncia"

[20] *Ibid.*

[21] "Danza de la muerte"

[22] in *Obras completas*, Vol. II, p. 1020 (translation mine).

[23] in *Obras completas*, Vol. II, p. 978.

TWO ASPECTS OF NATURE IN *LIBRO DE POEMAS:* NATURE AS THE LOST PARADISE AND NATURE AS TEACHER

Many are the authors who agree that external reality or Nature is the point of departure of most, if not all of Lorca's work.[1] Numerous also are the testimonies given by Lorca himself about Nature being the companion of his childhood years: "Mis más lejanos recuerdos de niño tienen sabor de tierra," says the poet in an interview with José R. Luna in 1934.[2] *Libro de poemas,* the first collection of poems written by Lorca between the ages of eighteen and twenty-two, is particularly relevant in this respect, as the poet himself indicates in the "Palabras de Justificación" at the beginning of the book: "Tendrá este libro la virtud, entre otras muchas que yo advierto, de recordarme en todo instante mi infancia apasionada correteando desnuda por las praderas de una vega sobre un fondo de serranía."[3]

He writes with his eyes and ears full of the exciting world around him, capturing it with visual images. He is attracted by the objects of his natural environment: bees, butterflies, common trees in the Andalusian countryside such as the black poplar or the oak, snails, frogs, cicadas and lizards. His is a world of proximity to all the creations of Nature.[4] Placing himself within a romantic tradition, the poet finds pleasure in projecting his subjectivity and most inner feelings into Nature. Nature, then becomes the sounding board for the poet's feelings. As Díaz-Plaja indicates: "El paisaje es solidario del goce y del dolor."[5] When echoing the poet's pessimistic and melancholic feelings, Nature is described as a lost paradise, faint image of his childhood paradise. At other times, the splendor and beauty of the world will emerge and impose itself forcing the poet to interrupt his introspective thoughts and to contemplate Nature. Nature's generosity, giving itself without recompense, sets an example for the poet to follow and establishes a source of hope. By following Nature's example, Lorca seems to comprehend the meaning of life.

I shall now try to analyze, especially through images, these two aspects of Nature in *Libro de poemas:* Nature as epitomizing Lorca's lost paradise and Nature as teacher.

Nature as the Lost Paradise

The general tone of *Libro de poemas* is one of melancholy and pessimism. The young poet is tortured by the beautiful memories of his childhood paradise, forever lost. He suffers desperately the dichotomy existing in his adult world, a dichotomy that can be best expressed by the words "wings-roots." Like Icarus, Lorca longs to reach the immensity of the Azure or firmament ("el Azul"), and to reestablish his communion with it. But now, the poet is hindered by the limitations of time and space that seem to control his adult reality. His consequent feeling of desolation is referred to as "pena blanca," for white is the emblem of sadness, and "nieve del alma"[6] that buries all passion and vitality. Also inherent in the symbolism of the color white are the elements of sterility and coldness, the latter better emphasized by the identification of sorrow with snow. His sorrow, acting as freezing snow, kills his vital impulses. As a parallel to his inner feelings, Nature appears to Lorca as "campo de nieve" and "cáliz de nieve," the former being repeated five times in the poem "Madrigal."

A whole series of metaphors give concrete form to a desolate and disenchanted world in which confusion dominates. "La sombra" is one of the most common images that allude to this lost Nature. It acquires different forms, such as "bruma," "niebla," "oscuridad," "borroso." In "Los encuentros de un caracol aventurero," Nature echoes the snail's confusion: "Todo estaba brumoso/de sol débil y niebla." The only light, the sun, is modified by a diminishing adjective, "débil" and defeated by the fog and the mist, images of the confusion the snail experiences in front of Nature and its message. The poet, like the snail, is unable to establish a direct contact with the world around him.

The image of "sombra" is often referred to as "ceniza" or

simply as "grís." In "Canción para la luna," the poet urges the moon to rebel against God, after which he announces the arrival of "el puro reino/de la ceniza." The poet's nihilism is represented by the image of "ceniza" as synonymous of a chaotic world. The presence or arrival of the shadow of confusion is often related to the image of the wind. The last verse in "Meditación bajo la lluvia," "El viento va trayendo a las sombras," sums up the confusion and desolation in which the poet finds himself.

In "Lluvia," the poet praises rain's fruitful values and admires the feeling of peace it brings to him: "Oh lluvia silenciosa, sin tormentas ni vientos." Like tempest, the winds are perturbing elements of which the fortunate rain is free. In "Aire de nocturno," the wind acquires a connotation of mysterious and disturbing premonition:

> ¿Qué es eso que suena
> muy lejos?
> Amor. El viento en las vidrieras,
> ¡amor mío!

This refrain, repeated three times in the poem, creates an atmosphere of unresolved suspense.

Another perturbing image presiding over this lost Nature is the spider. In "Patio húmedo," it appears as an image of time. Its web, with its "telares del siempre," petrifies, fixes everything into an inmobility very close to death. The poem opens and closes with two verses full of premonitions: "Las arañas/iban por los laureles." The laurels, symbol of glory and inmortality, are here invaded by the spider, image of time. Time destroys everything, the poet seems to say, including dreams of inmortality. In "Canción menor," the poet as well as Love, is covered by an inmense spider:

> El amor
> bello y lindo se ha escondido
> bajo una araña. El sol
> como otra araña me oculta
> con sus patas de oro.

All life is marked with the sign of time and death.

Walking with Nature, the poet converses with the trees and animals he finds on his way. They serve him as a sounding board for his questions and doubts about the meaning of his life in particular and the meaning of life in general. Nature as such serves only to echo Lorca's desperation. The trees, described as "flechas/caídas del Azul,"[7] reflect Lorca's sense of abandonment and his longing to reach the stars. They once belonged to infinity but like the poet, they are now exiled and forever longing for their place of origin. The black poplar is the tree with which the poet identifies the most. It is usually described by images that suggest authority and austerity: "Maestro," "Rudo abuelo del prado," "Pitágoras de la casta llanura."[8] Standing alone, abandoned by the rest of the forest, the black poplar epitomizes Lorca's solitude and isolation. In the poem "Chopo muerto," the poet describes the poplar's death through the use of a bisemic symbol. The suggestion created by the symbol is destroyed at the end by the poet himself, eager to manifest the identification between the poplar's natural demise and his own symbolic death:

> ¡Chopo viejo!
> . . .
> Yo te vi descender
> en el atardecer
> y escribo tu elegía,
> que es la mía.

The conscience of fleeting time and of the transitoriness of all existing things, is the main cause of the sand and melancholic tone of the book. Animals as well as inanimate things appear in dramatic effort to break the temporal and spatial limits enclosing them. In "Ritmo de otoño," the poet listens to the countryside that bitterly speaks to him. All in Nature confesses its lack of direction and its longing to go beyond the limits imposed by their own beings, in order to reach the Azure. The wind: "Y tengo la amargura solitaria/de no saber ni mi fin ni mi destino." The worms:

> -Soportamos tristezas
> al borde del camino.

> ...
> Dichosos los que nacen mariposas
> o tienen luz de luna en su vestido.

Life, as Gemma Roberts indicates, is viewed "como una serie infinita de posibilidades frustradas del Ser."[9]

Nature reflects the passage of time at a constant rhythm which Lorca describes as "la terrible noria del tiempo,"[10] or with a more mechanical image as a "tiovivo."[11] For the poet then, time is circular, limited in space but infinite in movement. It is a dynamic time that never stops. Sunset is therefore preferred above all other times of the day, for its sense of the transitory and the fleeting, for its lack of hope for a tomorrow. Sunsets seem to perpetuate time in its agony. In the poem "Campo," Lorca uses a sunset to reflect his own depression. In describing it, the poet resorts to the use of shades or nuances of colors in order to make them vague and ill defined. The effect is one of absolute desolation, purveyed by images such as: "cielo de ceniza," "árboles blancos," "Ocaso de sangre reseca," "monte incoloro," "fuentes turbias."

Nature as lost paradise echoes Lorca's feeling of himself as "angel caído,"[12] and he reveals his confusion and lack of direction in the outside world when he describes it as "selva," and "bosque sombrío."[13]

The world around is therefore viewed as "soledad/despintada por el llanto."[14] The tears refer to the "weeping" of the trees, that is, the falling of the leaves. Upon losing their leaves, the trees lose their color, and the scenery appears washed off, "despintada." The combination of the two images, the weeping of the trees and their lack of color or being washed off, portrays the very desolation and loneliness of the fall scenery.[15]

Nature as Teacher

As the contemplative person that he is, Lorca is entranced by the world of trees, flowers and animals. Nature's beauty and constant renewal are to him a message of life that he can not quite understand. He not only wishes to understand the Total Being of things, but he also longs to become one with it. According to Gemma Roberts: "Se trata de un ansia de posesión instigada por una capacidad de amor casi infinita; es decir, un deseo que no se satisface con el conocimiento, sino aspira a la identidad con el 'Ser'."[16] The poet is now like "el barbudo mago de los cuentos,"[17] speaking the language of flowers and trees, attending to the songs of the forest and identifying with its passionate yearnings. He is the devoted pupil, anxious to learn the lesson of Nature. The splendor of Nature seems to have been detained in an eternal morning, full of childish sweetness and simplicity.[18] Such a morning encourages Lorca to hope in a renewal like the one he perceives around him. The trees, always in attitude of prayer,[19] teach him a lesson of hope in the possibility of his regeneration. Once deaf to their songs, he is now able to perceive in the music of the trees the message from the Azure; their music comes from "el alma de los pájaros," "los ojos de Dios," and "la pasión perfecta."[20] En "Los encuentros de un caracol aventurero," the chosen ant is able to see the star only from the top of the highest tree, and for the snail's grandmother eternal life can only be found "sobre las hojas más tiernas/de los árboles más altos." Eager to understand Nature's message, the poet in "Manantial," grafts himself on to the centennial poplar hoping to be able to discover the secret of life the Nature seems to possess. In the evergreen oak the poet finds shelter and consolation. The oak has a symbolic and emblematic value of chastity and tranquil passion. Its fruit, the acorn, is "la serena/poesía de lo rancio."[21] The oak's song is the old song "con palabras de tierra entrelazadas/en la azul melodía." The oak tree brings back to him the elemental and simple characters of the poetry of the earth, the one he once knew as a child, strange to falseness and affectation. Under its shade, the poet renovates his hope of bringing to the surface "las esmeraldas líricas"[22] or poetical ability which lay latent inside of him.

Animals are also messengers of renewal. The bee is the one who will take the chosen ant to the star in "Los encuentros de un caracol aventurero." In their flying and buzzing, bees are the carriers of the yearning and exuberant life around. It is the cicada, above all, to which the poet addresses his hopeful call. He admires the cicada's death, "borracha de luz,"[23] pouring out sound, to be transfigured in celestial sound and light. The cicada symbolizes luminous death, long desired by the poet. A death which would free him from the danger of disappearing into nothingness. Rupert Allen indicates in the poem "Cigarra" a series of associations between the cicada, symbol and source of energy coming directly from God the sun, and Christ, son of God the Father and repository of his light.[24] The following lines:

> ¡Cigarra!
> ¡Dichosa tú! ,
> Pues te envuelve con su manto
> el propio Espíritu Santo,
> que es la luz.

correspond to the episode where, according to St. John, Rupert Allen continues, the Holy Ghost descended upon Christ from Heaven "and abode upon him." St. John also announces the arrival of the sun, that is, of Christ, into the world, who died enfolded in the mantle of the Holy Ghost. Again like Christ, the cicada after its death, is transfigured and returned to God. The same way that Christ's death and transfiguration entail man's salvation, the cicada, by capturing in itself the energy from the sun and transmitting it into sound, offers a model of a new and transfigurating being, fusion of terrestrial and spiritual elements, model for salvation. Before, the poet identified himself with the trees' yearning to reach the stars. In the cicada, he finds an example of communion with the Total Being:

> Sea mi corazon cigarra
> sobre los campos divinos.
> Que muera cantando lento
> por el ciel azul herido.[25]

The poet wishes to be a cicada over "the divine fields." Nature around, qualified by the adjective "divine," is endowed with the characteristics of paradise on earth or earthy heaven. Like the cicada that becomes the embodiment of a series of spiritual values, Nature becomes a reflection of the Azure, thanks to this yearning for participation in the Total Being of things, for a cosmic fusion that pervades all existing things.

Lorca pays particular attention to three elements in Nature: water, honey and the pomegranate. In them he sees the concrete representations of a series of moral and abstract values. They form a trilogy of life, purification and love. The poem "Mañana," sums up the vital, fruitful and purifying values of water. Everything in Nature dries and withers, but the song of the water endures forever: "Y la canción del agua/es una cosa eterna." In water the poet sees the reflection of the Azure. Water absorbs in itself the absolute quality of the firmament. In "Mañana," Lorca thus expresses it:

> Ella es firme y suave,
> llena de cielo y mansa.
> . . .
> Miel de luna que fluye
> de estrellas enterradas.

Water regenerates us, which comes from the idea of washing. In it, spirits clean themselves of all lies and corruption. In the above mentioned poem, the poet carries out the allegory water-Christ, where water, through the image of "luz hecha canto," is like God who in Christ became Word, song, and who lovingly gives himself to us at the Baptism. Like Christ in his Ascension, water goes up to heaven in white swaddling clothes, in the form of clouds. Water communicates God's love to Lorca. Water is also fruit and life: "Es la savia entrañable/que madura los campos," source of fertility, hence love that flows all meek and divine, for love is life and fruit. In the form of rain, water fills the countryside with fragments of the heavens whence it comes. Hope is renewed under the beneficial action of the rain: "Cuando sobre los campos desciendes lentamente/las rosas de mi pecho con tus sonidos abres."[26] In its elementary character, water regenerates the poet and takes him back to the lost paradise of his childhood. From water, he learns the lesson of openness and generosity as well as the confidence to aspire, like the knight of the popular song "Una tarde fresquita de Mayo," to reach the Azure through the paths of Nature.

In honey the poet finds the perfect balance between the material and spiritual. Honey unites within itself the most spiritual part of the flowers, the nectar, and for Lorca it is a liqueur of hope and love. He then compares it to the Host, synthesis of the body and blood of Christ. Like water, honey brings the poet back to his childhood. Honey is the realization of Lorca's ideal of harmonizing and uniting the conflicting tendencies that are tearing him apart.

The pomegranate is the vital symbol "par excellence," frantic explosion of life, the image of fertility and fruitful passion. In "Canción oriental," the poet carries out the allegory pomegranate-blood. Due to its color, the pomegranate suggests to Lorca the values of life and passion of which the blood is a carrier.

Water, honey and the pomegranate captivate the poet for their symbolical value of life and purification and the equilibrium of opposites, as well as fruitful passion. In these three elements the poet perceives fragments of the infinite, a part of God offered to him through Nature.

Many other elements in Nature, by participating of divine qualities, set an example for the poet. Kernels of wheat are "Cristo/en vida y muerte cuajado."[27] The wind is "sangre del infinito." In its soul "perdiéronse solemnes/carne y alma de Cristo."[28] And the spring of water

> Era un brotar de estrellas invisibles
> sobre la hierba casta,
> nacimiento del Verbo de la tierra
> por un sexo sin mancha.[29]

At the beginning of this paper I referred to the "Palabras de Justificación" that Lorca wrote as a preface to *Libro de poemas*. Childhood is there a happy memory connected to an open and paradisiacal Nature. To this childhood paradise the poet refers wistfully throughout the whole book. That childhood was the world of possibilities, the happy fusion between heaven and earth, a direct contact with the world around. With time, the world of happy continuity is replaced by that of painful separation: heaven recedes, relations between the poet and Nature grow colder. We have seen how Nature has been vivified and humanized by the poet who looks at it as the counterpart to his longings and fears. He has radiated his anxieties upon the natural elements. Nature has echoed his feelings of desperation when it too realizes the impossibility of penetrating the essence of the Total Being. Lorca's sorrow is a transcendental sorrow which he shares with the oak, the withered flower and the animals, for it is a part of their common destiny on earth. On one hand, Nature represents a hostile environment where only coldness and confusion exit. It is the lost paradise represented by images like "nieve," "sombras," "oscuridad," analyzed in the first part of this paper. But on the other hand, it is again through Nature that the poet regains hope and salvation. In its constant renewal, Nature has taught him the lesson of love and hope, the realization that the Total Being has to be sensed and not reasoned. Nature as teacher has helped Lorca accept himself and his human destiny. He longs now for a new heart:

> Corazón con arroyos
> y pinos,
> corazón sin culebras
> ni lirios.
> Robusto, con la gracia
> de un joven campesino
> que atraviesa de un salto
> el río.[30]

He wishes for an earthy heart, the heart of the simple and innocent man, the man with skin hardened by the sun,[31] so close to the nature of a child and hence so close to the Azure. His destiny is Nature, Mother Earth, where the secret of life and the accesibility of the stars are hidden. As M. T. Babín indicates: "En *Libro de poemas* predomina un pateísmo intenso en que la identidad con la naturaleza y el paisaje se hace una necesidad espiritual, un camino para llegar a Dios."[32] Rupert Allen affirms Lorca's belief that man's salvation must be realized tellurically. "Self-fulfillment must be realized in terms of a tellurically oriented consciousness."[33] That is why, as Rupert Allen indicates, Lorca sees his life as belonging to the world of the peasant, primary example of a being whose whole life is a commitment to the energy of Mother Earth.

The poet goes back to Nature, to the primitive and simple man. He wishes to contemplate Nature with the clear eyes of a child, and as such, to be able to speak to Nature directly. He wishes and hopes that his blood will fuse itself with earth and become fruitful mud:

> Y mi sangre sobre el campo
> sea rosado y dulce limo
> donde claven sus azadas
> los cansados campesinos.[34]

Only through a direct relationship with Nature can the poet be saved. God as salvation arrives through Nature. This puts us into an atmosphere of pantheism expressed in the identification of natural elements such as water, honey, cicada etc., with divine realities. This identification is possible because everything in Lorca's poetry is in constant fusion, thanks to a common yearning for a cosmic communion of all existing elements. All things share a common essence through which they can identify. Lorca's pantheism is then based on the belief that there is only one substance: the Total Being, absolute and eternal, and everything participates of it. That explains why all levels of reality touch and are equivalent: concrete things share cosmic and abstract values and earthly elements link with the stars. And as being-in-the-cosmos, man is too a part of that common essence.[35]

Candelas S. Newton
Wake Forest University

NOTES

[1]See: María Teresa Babín, *El mundo poético de Federico García Lorca* (San Juan de Puerto Rico: Biblioteca de Autores Puertorriqueños, 1954), 72, 77; Guillermo Díaz-Plaja, *Federico García Lorca* (Buenos Aires: Espasa-Calpe, 1955), 31; Edwin Honig, *García Lorca* (Norfolk: James Laughlin, 1944), 48; Roy Campbell, "The Early Poems," in *Lorca. A Collection of Critical Essays,* Manuel Durán, editor (Englewood Cliffs, New Jersey: Prentice-Hall, 1962), 66-67.

[2]Federico García Lorca, *Obras Completas* (Madrid: Aguilar, 1973), II, 958.

[3]All references to Lorca's poems are taken from Federico García Lorca, *Obras Completas* (Madrid: Aguilar, 1973), I.

[4]See Christoph Eich, *Federico García Lorca. Poeta de la intensidad* (Madrid: Gredos, 1958), 46.

[5]Díaz-Plaja, 36.

[6]García Lorca, "Canción de otoño," 15.

[7]García Lorca, "Arboles," 113.

[8]García Lorca, "In memoriam," 65; "El concierto interrumpido," 104.

[9]Gemma Roberts, "La intuición poética del tiempo finito en las *Canciones* de Federico García Lorca," *RHM,* 33 (1967), 256.

[10]García Lorca, "El diamante," 48.

[11]García Lorca, "Otro sueño," 132.

[12]García Lorca, "Mar," 129.

[13] García Lorca, "Los encuentros de un caracol aventurero," 10-11.

[14] García Lorca, "Noviembre," 69.

[15] See Jaroslaw M. Flys, *El lenguaje poético de Federico García Lorca* (Madrid: Gredos, 1955), 139.

[16] Gemma Roberts, 252.

[17] García Lorca, "Invocación al laurel," 135.

[18] García Lorca, "Los encuentros de un caracol aventurero," 9.

[19] García Lorca, "Los álamos de plata," 118.

[20] García Lorca, "Arboles," 113.

[21] García Lorca, "Canción oriental," 107.

[22] García Lorca, "Encina," 134.

[23] García Lorca, "Cigarra," 24.

[24] Rupert Allen, *The Symbolic World of Federico García Lorca* (Albuquerque: University of New Mexico Press, 1972), 38-42.

[25] García Lorca, "Cigarra," 25.

[26] García Lorca, "Lluvia," 35.

[27] García Lorca, "Canción oriental," 106.

[28] García Lorca, "Ritmo de otoño," 138.

[29] García Lorca, "Manantial," 124.

[30] García Lorca, "Prólogo," 89.

[31] García Lorca, "Encrucijada," 99.

[32] María Teresa Babín, 123.

[33] Rupert Allen, 38, 42.

[34] García Lorca, "Cigarra," 26.

[35] See Concha Zardoya, *Poesía española del siglo XX. Estudios temáticos y estilísticos* (Madrid: Gredos, 1974), 366-368.

NATURE AGAINST NATURE IN *YERMA*

Nature in *Yerma* means first of all the Granadine *vega* where Federico García Lorca was born. On the morning of July 17, 1936, he returned there, to the villa of his family, the Huerta de San Vicente, to celebrate Saint Frederick's Day with them and to spend, as he usually did, the summer away from Madrid.[1]

Arizonans are better placed than most North Americans to understand the qualities of the *vega*, where rich residual soil must contend with very little rainfall, so that irrigation is the age-old key to productivity. Water comes from both rivers and wells; and the region as a whole is reminiscent of that ancient Mediterranean culture, Babylonian, Egyptian, Tartessian, in which human effort is an essential part of the landscape, in contrast to North European and American perspectives, in which man would overwhelm, and is overwhelmed by, nature.[2] In the *vega*, the human presence is a kind of earthly grace that sustains the landscape which, without the labor of men, would lapse into waste.[3] And in a region where the husbandman, by constant, laborious ministrations supports the fruitfulness of the land, the relationship between the soil and the tiller of it becomes almost conjugal. Fertility results from frequent intercourse and from constant application of energy and will. Farmers in north temperate and tropical zones draw profit from nature's powerful impulses. The fruitfulness is there. They exploit it. In the *vega*, productivity is a potential, immanent in barrenness, which the farmer must learn to realize. Despite the good soil, the rivers, and the springs, sterility is the primordial situation, which the husbandman, by bringing water to the land reverses. In every sense, he is wedded to the earth.

And just as the Granadine peasant of the *vega* was literally conjugated with the earth, so, poetically, in his artistic toil, was Federico García Lorca. No statements of his are more often quoted than those celebrated ones called "El amor a la tierra,"

"Los arados Bravant," and "Complejo agrario." In them, Lorca outlines the major premise of his art:

> —Amo a la tierra—dice Lorca. Me siento ligado a ella en todas mis emociones. Mis más lejanos recuerdos de niño tiene sabor de tierra. La tierra, el campo, han hecho grandes cosas en mi vida. Los bichos de la tierra, los animales, las gentes campesinas, tienen sugestiones que llegan a muy pocos. Yo las capto ahora con el mismo espíritu de mis años juveniles...[4]

He then proceeds to recall how a new kind of steel plow, furrowing deeply into the soil, turned up a Roman mosaic with an inscription that he associates with Daphnis and Chloe. The event was, in 1906, an artistic awakening for the poet: "Mis primeras emociones están ligadas a la tierra y a los trabajos del campo. Por eso hay en mi vida un complejo agrario, que llamarían los psicoanalistas. Sin este mi amor a la tierra, no hubiera podido escribir *Bodas de sangre.* Y no hubiera tampoco empezado mi obra próxima: *Yerma.*"

Twice Lorca here describes his link with the soil as an emotional bond: "ligado." This connection might also be described as marital. Yet once again one must discriminate. Lorca's earth is not a northern force of nature, not the savage vitality that blurs and chokes the rational order of a formal garden in Pardo-Bazán's *Los Pazos de Ulloa*[5] or the bloody battle of Sedan fought in all its horror in the August midst of Zola's "éternelle et souriante nature."[6] His earth is a desert that husbandry has brought to bloom. Such a landscape is already a human work of art, and it is small wonder that the plow that probes more profoundly would turn up a classical Mediterranean artifact. The entire arable extent of Lorca's poetic domain is in fact studded with *objets trouvés*, experience with the finish and style of highly crafted art. Yet at the root of his whole flowering is a barrenness out of which a willed, laborious and conscious poetry grows. As García Lorca himself has observed, *Bodas de sangre* and *Yerma* are similar growths. In *Bodas,* the Novia's father has created their livelihood by transforming a waste into a productive farm: "...no es buena tierra; pero con los brazos se la hace buena...."[7] The very locus of *Bodas* is the *secanos,* where one must practice dry farming, the *cultivo de secano* which characterizes nearly a third of Spanish agriculture. Likewise,

Lorca's art is a *cultivo de secano*. To be sure, Lorca was rather more favored, as is the Novio in *Bodas de sangre*, with respect to both his agricultural and artistic inheritance. The *vega* has irrigation. Lorca came from a gifted family. Nonetheless, the raw material in both lines of transmission is waste, desert. In such a perspective, the title of the play *Yerma* assumes a fresh significance, a Mallarméan intensity. Like the French poet's wintry whiteness of the icy page as yet unwritten upon, *Yerma* presents us with the barren earth that is the essence and the precondition of Lorca's Andalusian art. Thus the fundamental function of the play is to examine sterility in terms of fertility, and exuberance from the vantage point of repression, to explore the paradoxical relations between want and excess. For one major phase of the tragedy of Yerma is that, in the midst of productive and reproductive plenty, she alone appears to be lacking:

> Que estoy ofendida, ofendida y rebajada hasta lo último viendo que los trigos apuntan, que las fuentes no cesan de dar agua y que paren las ovejas cientos de corderos, y las perras, y que parece que todo el campo puesto de pie me enseña sus crías tiernas, adormiladas, mientras yo siento dos golpes de martillo aquí en lugar de la boca de mi niño. (1317-18)

Lorca makes it quite clear that Yerma's husband Juan is deficient as a sire. In the first place he is perfectly content with their childlessness, because of which they live more abundantly: "Las cosas de la labor van bien, no tenemos hijos que gasten" (1275). Perhaps even more significantly, in a conversation just previous to this statement, Juan rejects all the little attentions that Yerma would like to press upon him. These are maternal, and in avoiding them, he negates the concept of maternity that would, through Yerma, see himself reproduced in a son. The little attentions anticipate the son, conjure him. In refusing them, Juan refuses him, just as he refuses the seminally white glass of milk that Yerma suggests, much as in *Bodas de sangre* the Novio does not care to take the lunch his mother would prepare. There is, in the speech of the Vieja in act I, a suggestion that the trouble with Juan may be biological. When the old woman refuses to give Yerma advice, Yerma declares that God will then have to help her. The Vieja then denies the existence of God, but wishes that he might be a reality so that he could "mandara rayos contra los hombres de simiente podrida que encharcan la alegría de los campos" (1291). The husband's seed is, then, rotten. But in the play's final exchange between Yerma and Juan, the physiological takes on a psychological hue. Juan wills for Yerma not to conceive a child: "Yerma. ¿Y nunca has pensado en él cuando me has visto desearlo? Juan. Nunca. Yerma. ¿Y no podré esperarlo? Juan. No." (1349).

This ambivalent refusal of Juan's, apparently both physical and mental, to sire a child on a wife who above all else desires to be a mother has struck critics as a weakness in *Yerma,* occasioning Valbuena Prat to observe that the work should rather be called *Yermo.*[8] Like the Vieja, many students of the play would perhaps opine that "La culpa es de tu marido" (1344). And since no critic has yet, so far as I know, offered a convincing explanation of Juan's denial, it does come to seem like a serious fault in one of Lorca's most powerful dramas. One can understand Yerma's murder of her husband, but his obstinate refusal to give her what she so passionately wants remains unclear.[9]

Juan's progress in the play may provide a clue. At its beginning we see him as cunning husbandman: "Las cosas de la labor van bien." And when Víctor comes upon Yerma sewing and mistakenly thinks that the garments are for the child, he relates Juan's farming skills to the absence of offspring in the house: "Dile a tu marido que piense menos en el trabajo. Quiere juntar dinero y lo juntará pero ¿a quién lo va a dejar cuando se muera?" We then learn that Juan's flock, together with his fields, is on the increase: "Yo me voy con las ovejas. Dile a Juan que recoja las dos que me compró, ye en cuanto a lo otro, ¡que ahonde!" (1285).

Here again, Víctor couples Juan's success with Yerma's want. This theme reappears at a deeper level of intensity when Víctor calls on Yerma and Juan to take leave of them, at the end of Act II. Yerma's despair is at this moment so great that she has resolved to seek the help of the witch Dolores. She then learns, to her great surprise, that Juan has bought all of Víctor's sheep. In the eyes of Víctor and Yerma both, the transfer is something on the order of a biblical benediction. He says: "Tu marido ha de ver su hacienda colmada." And she rejoins. "El fruto viene a las manos del trabajador que lo busca" (1324). What

Yerma and Juan now have is superabundance. Juan according observes: "Ya no tenemos sitio donde meter tantas ovejas." Yet Yerma's cruel deprivation is the companion to Juan's triumphant multiplication. Carlos Rincón interprets Juan's activity as a modern, commercial kind of activity.[10] I see in *Yerma* not a shred of evidence to support that view. Juan's fruitfulness is ancient and Old-Testamentary, a proliferation of land, crops and beasts. As he flowers, Yerma withers: "¡Marchita!" The relationship, then, between husband and wife is an inverse one. The more he prospers, the deeper her despair. It is when Juan accompanies the shorn Víctor for a short distance that Yerma slips off to Dolores' house, to implore fecundity. Her final act, the most despairing of all, is to make the fatal pilgrimage. Juan's wealth is, all the while, at its peak, "colmada." In this cruel inverse conjugation of the husband's abundance with the wife's scarcity one already discerns so considerable a calculation of art that "weakness" no longer seems an idea applicable to the situation. Nonetheless, its precise nature remains difficult to make out.

To clarify, one should perhaps begin with tillage, which García Lorca has called his "primer asombro artístico (1755)." We have already seen that the share does not break the Andalusian earth to release its energies but rather to cause its barrenness to fructify. A basic Mediterranean (and other) association with plowing is sexual intercourse. Cervantes, in quite another context, makes just such a connection when Don Quijote, in his great discourse in recollection of the Golden Age, describes nature before the Fall of man: "aún no se había atrevido la pesada reja del corvo arado a abrir ni visitar las entrañas piadosas de nuestra primera madre, que ella, sin ser forzada, ofrecía, por todas partes de su fértil y espacioso seno, lo que pudiese hartar, sustentar y deleitar a los hijos que entonces la poseían."[11] Indeed, Don Quijote makes a number of audacious links in this description. But his main image in connection with agriculture is that the plowshare's entry into the earth, after the Fall, is an act of sexual force, a rape. Rather more subtly, Lorca himself introduces sexuality into the first "asombro" with his mention of Daphnis and Chloe. The Daphnis of Longus' romance was named after "a mythic personage named Daphnis. He had been exposed in a laurel grove, was raised by shepherds, was taught by Pan to play the pipes, became a beloved of Apollo, and invented pastoral poetry."[12] Moreover, the story of Longus' *Daphnis and Chloe* notably concerns itself with sexual awakening in the female and the male. Thus Lorca's experience in 1906 was both an artistic and a sexual illumination. Art and sexuality are very closely associated in his mind; and both emanate from the furrowed earth, forming a complex, an ensemble, "un complejo agrario, que llamarían los psicoanalistas." Something of the phallic quality of this complex may be perceived in the poet's descriptions. He remembers the new plow by name, Bravant, recalls how it had won prizes for its "eficacia," calls it "vigoroso," mentions his pleasure in seeing "cómo la enorme púa de acero abría un tajo en la tierra, tajo del que brotaban raíces en lugar de sangre" (1755).

The phallic plow working in conjunction with the imperatives of art is hardly original with García Lorca, although its impress upon him in 1906 created a unique configuration. Shakespeare himself deals with the themes of sterility and fertility as, in the first seventeen of his sonnets, he calls upon a beautiful young man to propagate his beauty by stiring offspring in wedlock. Thus exhorting him, Shakespeare takes the line that loveliness should perpetuate itself in an unbroken succession: "From fairest creatures we desire increase/that thereby beauty's rose might never die." The difficulty is that the young man is narcissistically self-absorbed, wed to himself; "But thou, contracted to thine own bright eyes,/Feed'st thy light's flame with self-substantial fuel,/Making a famine where abundance lies." Here also the image of want in the midst of plenty reappears, as it does when the poet chides: "And, tender churl, makest waste in niggarding."[13] Shakespeare's remedy, advanced for aesthetic reaons, is marriage and a child:

> Look on thy glass, and tell the face thou viewest
> Now is the time that face should form another,
> Whose fresh repair if now thou not renewest,
> Thou dost beguile the world, unbless some mother.
> For where is she so fair whose uneared womb
> Disdains the tillage of thy husbandry?
> Or who is he so fond will be the tomb
> Of his self-love, to stop posterity?[14]

In *Yerma,* as in these sonnets of Shakespeare, we have great human beauty. The Vieja cherishes Yerma's loveliness, and regrets its waste: "Buenos [días] los tenga la hermosa muchacha. . ." " ¡Ay, qué flor abierta! Qué criatura tan hermosa eres" (1286, 1290). But, even in the context of marriage, even in the tillage of Juan's husbandry, Yerma is unblessed as a mother because, somehow, Juan has stopped posterity.

I would offer two explanations, one artistic, the other ritualistic. Shakespeare hints at the adverse effect which aesthetics has on biology. His youth is "contracted to thine own bright eyes," intent upon the self. A preoccupation with beauty can and does produce a deep involvement with inner processes that makes the person so preoccupied negligent of others. Creative artists tend to be poor spouses and worse parents. Juan is certainly no creator in the usual sense. Yet, outside the home, he propagates splendidly, increasing all his possessions. In his private life, however, all is barrenness, his wife childless, his sisters spinsters. We find the same contradiction in the structure of Bernarda Alba's existence. She cruelly cloisters her daughters, but has a gift for animal husbandry, so that the visiting neighbor Prudencia, when she hears the stallion's commotion, is compelled to observe: "Has sabido acrecentar tu ganado" (1508). And Bernarda, while trying to keep all the men away from her house and daughters, plans to release the stallion among the new mares at dawn.

Among the artists one finds those who are prodigal of their talents and those who are niggardly of them. Niggardly artists have a sense of personal limitation. One reason Henry James did not marry was that his little income was just sufficient to sustain one person, but not a family.[15] Hemingway felt that the well of creativity should never be emptied in the day, that enough should be left to prime the flow of invention on the morrow. He also believed that each man had a limited number or orgasms.[16] There are spendthrift writers but many more, I would suppose, who preserve and protect their creative substance, even though they produce major amounts of work. Indeed, this relative sterility is interpreted by them as contributing to their productivity. Balzac believed that his vast output was in some measure connected with celibacy; and many of his most energetic characters, for good or for ill, are unmarried, Bette Fischer of *La Cousine Bette,* for example, whose parsimony fundamentally contrasts with the extravagance of the Baron Hulot d'Ervy in that novel.[17] Yerma's Juan may be taken as a Lorquean analogue of the artist who, to be able to create in breadth and depth, only grudgingly expends sexually a vital substance: "Cuando me cubre cumple con su deber, pero yo le noto la cintura fría, como si tuviera el cuerpo muerto. . ." (1329).

Juan's art and his offspring are of course the vineyards, flocks and fields that give forth and multiply as an inverse function of his abstention from the will to propagate in his own marriage bed. The seed that might bring forth the child fertilizes his beasts and plants instead. Yerma's famine feeds their abundance. The fertilizing effect of abstention is not merely a poetic or novelistic intuition. In human reproduction, the spermatazoa in the male increase after abstinence, thus improving the woman's chances of conceiving. Similarly, *Yerma* surrounds the scant and impotent ejaculations of Juan at home with the images rich in suggestions of seminal abundance abroad. When Yerma imagines the child she hopes to nurse, milk is the inexhaustible product of semen: "Yo tengo la idea de que las recién paridas están como iluminadas por dentro y los niños se duermen horas y horas sobre ellas, oyendo ese arroyo de leche tibia que les va llenando los pechos para que ellos mamen, para que ellos jueguen hasta que no quieran más, hasta que retiren la cabeza: 'Otro poquito más, niño,' y se les llena la cara y el pecho de gotas blancas" (1327-8). Want never dreamed a richer dream of plenty, but the arroyo brings to mind other such associations that together form a *complejo reproductivo*. Often in Lorca unimpeded sexuality takes the form of free-flowing waters, the river in contrast to the well, pond, cistern or pool. Or the foaming sea. Lorca's liberated waters are white waters. On land, sheep often create the effect of the ocean's or of the river's foaming richness. In *Yerma*, sheep are originally associated with Víctor, the man naturally formed to impregnate Yerma. The first frame of Act II occurs at the river, with the women washing and gossiping about Juan, Víctor and Yerma. The fourth Lavandera catches sight of the sheep on their way to pasture and, bringing together a multiplicity of seminal images, describes their advance: "una inundación de lana. Arramblan con todo" (1306). The verb *arramblar* especially suggests the whiteness of rapids, the emotional wealth of that inexhaustive sexuality of which Yerma is deprived.

Ritual is the reason for her deprivation. Yerma is sacrificed, as we realize when she speaks of her cross, her stigmata, and also when her friend urges her to remember the wounds of our Lord. By stopping her posterity, Juan magically assures the fertility of the agricultural world that he controls. His technique is to prune, *podar,* at home, so that away from it the fields will flower and the trees bear fruit. It would perhaps have been possible to use purely sympathetic magic, impelling the crops to produce on the model of his and Yerma's offspring. But Juan has learned how to channel the forces of abstinence from the human to the agricultural scene, so that he spends all night irrigating rather than in his wife's embrace. This deflected force marvellously quickens the processes of nature at Yerma's expense. Her barrenness guarantees their vitality. And when Yerma at last realizes that she is contracted to this enduring rite of exploitation, she acquires a vengefully celibate masculine strength that enables her to throttle her husband. For Juan has used nature against nature. And Yerma's tragedy now is that, with Juan, her last desperate hope for a child has also died: "he matado a mi hijo" (1350). Yet in the final analysis, Juan's sterile humanity, at the same time that it is responsible for Yerma's tragedy, is also responsible for the great and moving work of dramatic art that is *Yerma,* the play. From the waste of two lives, a world of art has been made to flower, perversely perhaps, but also revealingly, as Federico García Lorca presents to us the fearful affinities between barrenness and fertility, in both the human and the natural scene. So *Yerma* paradoxically conjugates the parsimonious with the prodigal in a truly prodigious play.[18]

Robert Ter Horst
University of Arizona

NOTES

[1] Ian Gibson, *The Death of Lorca* (Chicago, 1973), 45-51.

[2] In the *Discours de la méthode,* Descartes plans for man to "nous rendre comme maîtres et possesseurs de la nature."

[3] Among the sources I have consulted are the Encyclopedia Britannica entries on Granada and Spain.

[4] From the 1971 edition in Aguilar of the *Obras completas* (1954-55). All further citations from the work of García Lorca, including interviews and statements, are of this edition.

[5] *Los pazos de Ulloa,* (Mexico, 1958), p. 31.

[6] Emile Zola, *La débâcle,* I (Paris: Charpentier, n.d.), p. 240.

[7] Aguilar, p. 1197. Also p. 1196: "En mi tiempo, ni esparto daba esta tierra. Ha sido necesario castigarla y hasta llorarla, para que nos dé algo provechoso."

[8] Quoted in Carl Cobb, *Federico García Lorca* (Boston: Twayne, 1967), p. 136.

[9] I am loath to accept purely mythic interpretations of *Yerma,* because they tend to generalize and attenuate the clear, specific, and precise economy of the play itself. In these last works for the theatre, Lorca is moving away from abstraction to a new nominalism, as the very titles *Doña Rosita, Yerma* and *Bernarda Alba* attest. Thus the conclusion of Patricia F. Sullivan's "The Mythic Tragedy of *Yerma,*" *Bulletin of Hispanic Studies* XLIX (1972), 265-75, seems to me unsatisfactory because of its lifeless generalization, as well as retrograde in terms of the poet's progress:

> ". . .the tragic resolution of the play is the inevitable outcome of Yerma's sterility within her mythic conception as Mother-Earth.

Her sterility, in turn, is a result of Juan's spiritual poverty regarding the desire for children. . . All hope for any kind of integration into the cosmic rhythm dissolves when Yerma realizes definitely that Juan desires *not* to have children. Bereft of any mythic justification for her marriage, Yerma destroys the Sky-God and, with him, the Mother-Earth she might have been (p. 278).

[10] *Das Theater García Lorcas* (Berlin, 1975), 269-70.

[11] *Don Quijote de la Mancha,* ed. Martín de Riquer (Barcelona, 1966), p. 105.

[12] Arthur Heiserman, *The Novel Before the Novel* (Chicago, 1977), p. 134.

[13] Sonnet 1 in *Shakespeare, The Complete Works,* ed. G. B. Harrison (New York, 1952), p. 1595.

[14] Harrison, Sonnet 3, p. 1595.

[15] See Leon Edel's *Henry James, The Conquest of London 1870-1881* (New York, 1963), 345-46. The reasons go deeper, doubtless, than these superficial ones; but preservation surely also reflects this deeper sense.

[16] Ernest Hemingway, *A Moveable Feast* (New York: Bantam, 1970), p. 26: "I had learned never to empty the well of my writing, but always to stop when there was still something there in the deep part of the well, and let it refill at night from the springs that fed it."

Carlos Baker, *Ernest Hemingway, A Life Story* (New York, 1969), p. 205: "Ernest began expounding his views on male sexuality. A young man should make love very seldom, said he, or he would have nothing left for middle ages. The number of available orgasms was fixed at birth and could be expended too soon."

A perhaps even more revealing statement is one Hemingway made to Charles Scribner, directly relating a limited sexuality to a limited creativity. See Baker, p. 465: In June of 1948, Hemingway "sent Charles Scribner a series of letters full of down-to-earth family gossip, including the statement that he always had to ease off on making love when he was working hard because the two things were run by the same motor."

[17] The Bette of *La cousine Bette* is, like *Yerma,* a study in frustration, both of the sexual and maternal instincts. Bette is passionately devoted to the weakling Swedish sculptor Wenceslas Steinbock. Her frustration, however, takes the form of cruel and calculated revenge. She is an inverse creator.

[18] But not one without parallel. Eugene O'Neill's *Strange Interlude* (New York, 1928), perhaps even more brilliantly studies the female's striving for biological self-realization, with a first phase of sterility followed by fecundity and bitter triumph over the male.

IMAGERY OF NATURE AND ITS FUNCTION IN LORCA'S POETIC DRAMA: "REYERTA" AND *BODAS DE SANGRE*

> Broken flowers their eyes, and their teeth
> two fistfuls of hardened snow.
> Both of them fell, and the bride returns,
> stained with blood, tresses and skirt.
> Covered with two blankets they come
> carried on the shoulders of tall young men.
> So it was. Nothing more. It was just.
> Upon the flower of gold, impure sand.[1]

With these words the Beggar Woman of *Blood Wedding* dispatches summarily with the violent and senseless death of the two young men. Their blood now dark and dried on the skirt and tresses of the Bride, Leonardo and his adversary are borne home on the shoulders of other tall young men. Their eyes are crushed flowers; their teeth, two handfuls of crusted snow; their bodies, an armful of desiccated *flora* (1276). And yet, this tragic bloodshed is seen as just, or simply as that which was to be expected, nothing more: lowly sand cast upon the flower of life in its moment of fullest vital potential, the harvesting by Death of wheat in its prime and before it has released its seed to the wind. The callous matter-of-factness of this dismissal of the tragedy as something unworthy of that name, as something that is little more than another detail of everyday business is not unique in Lorca. To the contrary, it is in consonance with his fatalism in general and echoes in particular a similar attitude that pervades his *Romancero gitano*. As an example, let me refer momentarily to the ballad "Reyerta" (variously rendered as "Fracas," "Scuffle" and "Vendetta"—the last of which most faithfully conveys the nature of this "battle"), in which the victims of another knife-fight lie dead or dying in the evening light while the judge called to witness the scene comments dispassionately to the Civil Guards accompanying him:

> Gentlemen of the Civil Guard,
> here has occurred what has always occurred:
> four dead Romans
> and five Carthaginians.   (429)

For the judge of "Reyerta," as for Death in *Blood Wedding*, there is little to be disturbed about. Nothing surprising has happened; it is merely an extension of what has always been and will always be. Like the victim of *Blood Wedding*, the wounded horsemen of "Reyerta" meet their end in a struggle whose repetition and outcome appear to be as predictable as the setting of the sun or the autumn harvest. Indeed, it is Lorca's view of men as integral parts of the natural cycle—albeit parts that are self-conscious and reluctant—that provides the source of irony and tension fundamental to the "tragedy" of play and poem alike. And it is precisely the usage and interweaving of the natural world—*i.e.*, the unconscious and ongoing progression of the days or the seasons—with the separately self-conscious world of men that sets the stage for resultant conflict and apparent tragedy.

Just what *is* the relationship of setting to event, of macro- to micro-cosmic dimension, that produces this paradoxical comment on the nature of our existence? In brief, it is the casting of human comings and goings against the much larger backdrop of planetary movement or the eternal rotation of the sessions that yields this effect. In the case of "Reyerta," it is virtually impossible to extricate and disentangle the supposed gypsy knife-fight from the celestial setting of eventide or to distinguish and satisfactorily between that which is above from that which is below. Lorca called these ballads new "myths of [his] own invention," (1598) and through the eye of a "primitive" mentality we are witnessing the explanation or rendering of human death and violence in terms of the natural imagery of a sunset simultaneously with a cosmic event that is described in anthropomorphic terms. The interweaving of the two is so thorough—as indeed it is in many of the ballads of this collection—that the only conclusion to be reached is that for Lorca the inclusion of one as part of the reality of the other was the ultimate comment on the nature of human struggle and defeat at the hands of the inevitable.

We should look briefly at "Reyerta" with the foregoing in mind. A "harsh light of playing cards" illuminates the scene and sets a tone of fatal predestination for the ensuing conflict: it is "in the cards" and is given almost ritual overtones in the form of ageless old women who witness the event and in that of ministering angels, black and with ice-water compresses, that appear in the western sky:

> A harsh light of playing cards
> etches against the bitter green
> infuriated stallions
> and the profiles of riders.
> . . . .
> Black angels were bringing
> compresses of water and snow.
> Angels with long wings,
> like the knives of Albacete.   (429)

One Juan Antonio el de Montilla rolls down the slope of the cliffside with wounds like pomegranates at his temples to "mount a cross of fire/on the road to death" (429), a direct allusion to the setting sun, the daily victim of a cosmic vendetta that is as "real" and predictable as the clash of passions among men. There is no reason for surprise, then, when the judge views the homicide as just another instance of that which has carried men to their death from time immemorial: another conflict of wills, another battle, and resultant death. It is we, who as spectators and participants, impute a "tragicness" to an event that is otherwise as uncomplicated as the completion of another rotation of the earth or the coming of winter. Failing light finds the wounded thighs of the horsemen while black angels—the last of evening clouds—keep vigil and close the ballad with a sense of timelessness and detachment from the supposed human event, leaving the reader to ponder just what it is that has happened:

> The afternoon mad with fig trees
> and warm mumurings
> falls in a faint upon the wounded thighs
> of the horsemen.
> And black angels were flying
> in the western sky.
> Angels with long tresses
> and hearts of oil.   (429)

Tempting is a comparison with a similar rendering of sunrise by Antonio Machado:

> The canvas of the eastern sky
> was bleeding tragedies,
> daubed
> with grotesque clouds.[2]

It has been remarked, and quite exactly so, that Lorca's poetry is dramatic and his theater, poetic. This intermingling of the narrative and the lyric no doubt finds its high point, on the one hand, in *Romancero gitano* and, on the other, in *Blood Wedding*. Whereas "Reyerta" is essentially poetry in dramatic form, *Blood Wedding* is drama cast in highly lyrical terms. It is this lyricism along with the central motif of the planting, cultivating and reaping of crops that carries the impact of the play from the individual to the universal, from the concrete to the abstract. From the very first words of the play forward the identity of men with the world of nature in the larger sense is patent. For the Mother her slain husband and son were "two geraniums" (1173) and in a variation of the refrain "el pan, pan y el vino, vino" she makes the implicit comparison of men to wheat when she exclaims to the Groom, "Your grandad left a son on every street corner. That's what I like! Men should be men and wheat, wheat (Los hombres, hombres; el trigo, trigo.)" (1174). At the same time it is she who insists on the evil of any agent of "destruction"—be it one of pruning, slaughtering or the harvest:

> Machetes, knives. . .damn them all and the idiot that invented them. . . . And shotguns, pistols and the smallest pocket knife and even the hoes and pitchforks of the threshing floors. . . . Anything that can cut the body of a man. A man with grace, with all his flower in his mouth. . . . Your father, who smelled like a carnation. . . . Is it just, can it be that something so small, the size of a pistol or a knife, can be the end of a man? A man with all the beauty of a bull? (1173)

And at the end of scene I a friend who has come to visit tells the Mother that a neighbor's son has had both arms cut off by the reaping machine.

The apparent conflict here is between the metaphoric vision

of men as wheat, geraniums, bulls, carnations, etc., and the horror shown toward the instruments for reaping them. The paradox is double when one considers that these people take their livelihood from the soil and spend no little energy in ensuring future well-being by marriages of convenience that would join one "capital" with another or bring "water" to the badlands. This intention is evident in the third scene of Act I when the marriage arrangements are made between the Mother of the Groom and the Father of the Bride in the arid wastelands of the latter:

> Groom: These are the badlands.
>
> Mother: Your father would have covered them with trees.
>
> Groom: With no water?
>
> Mother: He would have found it. The three years we were married he planted ten cherry trees, the three walnuts by the mill and a whole vineyard... (1195)

And it is the Bride who says at the beginning of Act II that "[her] mother was from a place that had a lot of trees" (1206). For the Mother the marriage is the "turning over of earth, the planting of new trees" (1240), and throughout the act the wedding song abounds in natural imagery such as "boughs in flower," "platters of wheat," "laurel in bloom," "trays of dahlias," "orange blossoms," "flower of gold," etc. By Act III and the tragic denouement the identification between human events and happenings in nature is so complete that when the Mother speaks of the recently slain son as an "armful of dried flowers" (1267) or the "sunflower of [his] mother" (1270) the affective usage of vegetal terms has become so customary that it no longer evokes surprise as metaphor. The Bride describes the ease of ending her life as "less trouble than clipping off a dahlia of [the Mother's] flower garden" (1270), and at the very end of the play the tininess of a knife blade has sought out the mooring place of life at the very center of its self-consciousness "where entangled trembles/the dark root of anguish" (1272). The question posed by the Mother at the beginning of the work—"And is it just...that a tiny thing like...a knife can end the life of a man?"—is answered dispassionately by the Beggar Woman in the last scene, "So it was. Nothing more. It was just./Upon the flower of gold, impure sand" (1267). The Groom was, after all, only "a tiny bit of water," "a dash of cold water" (1269) compared to the "dark river" represented by Leonardo and his horse. What other outcome was to be expected? Given the careful and consistent interweaving of human and natural events, the absence of a sense of tragedy in conventional terms and the remove at which Death comments on her own doings, one might just as well ask the question, "Is is just for a tree to die?"

Whatever tragedy is present would seem to lie more in the meaninglessness of it all and in the certainty of its repetition than in the event in and of itself. Much the same as in "Reyerta," we appear to have witnessed simply one more performance of an ongoing show, a show to be enacted with the same regularity as that of sunset or the harvesting of wheat. The inclusion of man as another element in nature predestined to be the victim of its own passions causes us to wonder if it is tragic that we are the way we are of if the true "tragedy" lies in our attempts and failures at controlling what is apparently and essentially uncontrollable.

David K. Loughran
University of Montana

NOTES

[1] Federico García Lorca, *Obras completas,* ed. Arturo del Hoyo, (Madrid, 1965), p. 1266. All other page references will appear in text directly following quotations. The translations are mine.

[2] Antonio Machado, *Poesías* (Buenos Aires, 1962), p. 54, "El cadalso."

IMAGERY AND THEME IN
EL MALEFICIO DE LA MARIPOSA

The purpose of this paper is to examine some of Lorca's early images and the context in which they were first introduced. These images support attitudes and concerns which tend to recur in this author and valuable insights can be gained by considering those images he retains as well as those he abandons for given periods of time.

Many critics have stressed the fact that Lorca was a conscientious artist who chose his images with great care.[1] The poet himself expressed what seemed like a guiding principle when, in his conference on Góngora, he stated:

> la metáfora está siempre regida por la vista (a veces por una vista sublimada), pero es la vista la que la hace limitada y le da su realidad (*O.C.*, I, p. 1008)[2]

He confessed, then, to a basic reliance on observation which provided him with a firm scaffold, un "seguro andamio de madera" (*O.C.*, II, 1221), grounded in reality from where he could capture the essentials and transform them into poetic substance.

In this first period the object observed is the world of nature, and from it Lorca extracts images he develops in his early poetry and in his first play. Our guide, as we penetrate this early imagery, will be *El maleficio de la mariposa (The Spell of the Butterfly)*, a two-act play in verse which opened in Madrid in March 22, 1920 and which introduced this author to theatrical audiences. Lorca had originally titled it "La menor de las comedias,"[3] perhaps ironically contrasting the child-like perspective and the miniature world presented in the play to the world and perspectives found in the "alta comedia" of the times. Gregorio Martínez Sierra, who was then director of the Eslava theater where the work premiered, suggested the new title.[4] It seems that plays about magic or plays based on fairy tales were popular with Spanish audiences at that particular period[5] and Martínez Sierra, being a man of considerable theatrical experience, probably surmised that the new title would attract more public. We do know that Lorca agreed to the new name but with some misgivings.[6]

The intriguing title, musical excerpts from Grieg and Debussy and even a dance sequence by a noted artist did not help the play. It failed. Alfredo de la Guardia recalls in his book that the actors had to contend with a unruly audience from the beginning:

> Desde butacas, palcos y localidades altas se prodigaron los denuestos, las frases contundentes, que se cruzaban como chispas sobre el rumor sordo del taconeo, vigorizado por los bastones. En vano aquí y allá unos cuantos espectadores—escritores, artistas —clamaron "¡Queremos escuchar la obra!" La tempestad fue en aumento y ni siquiera Catalina Bárcena pudo contener a los albo rotadores.[7]

As a result, it closed the next day and was never edited. An incomplete manuscript appeared for the first time in the 1954 Aguilar edition of the *Obras Completas*. The recent 1974 edition adds a few more lines supplied by André Belamich, but the manuscript is still incomplete.

El maleficio is unusual in that it is an "insect play," that is, its main characters are "curianas" or cockroaches. A butterfly, a scorpion and a few glowworms complete the cast. Conscious of the fact that animals, let alone insects, were not traditional to the Spanish stage, Lorca used the prologue to justify their presence:

> ¿Y por qué a vosotros los hombres, llenos de pecados y de vicios incurables, os inspiran asco los buenos gusanos que se plasean tranquilamente por la pradera tomando el sol en la mañana tibia? ¿Qué motivo tenéis para despreciar lo ínfimo de la Naturaleza? Mientras que no améis profundamente a la piedra y al gusano no entraréis en el reino de Dios. (*O.C.*, II, p. 6)

Lorca was using the insects to voice a message of reconciliation and love. Man needed to learn to love all things, to be humble. After all, he too was a creature of God, and it was the poet's responsibility to remind him of that truth. All of these ideas were explicit in the prologue:

> . . .di poeta, a los hombres que el amor nace con la misma intensidad en todos los planos de la vida; . . .dile al hombre que sea humilde, ¡todo es igual en la Naturaleza! (*O.C.*, II, p. 6)

The insects, repugnant and unlovable, were to call attention to the forgotten ones, the outcasts in society but at the same time, their acts would parallel the acts of man. They were basically terrestrial creatures bound to an earthly existence same as man.

Lorca had already shown concern for the human condition and for human needs in his first book in prose, *Impresiones y paisajes,* where he had also shown a keen sensitivity towards suffering of any kind, be it of man or beast. A message of reconciliation was especially topical in a society which was showing signs of the fragmentation that would eventually lead to the Civil War. The explicit message also served the structural need for a lesson or "moraleja" in a play about animals. Most of all, Lorca seemed bent in calling attention to the dogmatic intolerance of some who tended to mutilate life by stressing certain aspects of reality at the exclusive of other aspects, a theme that had also appeared in his first book in prose in the section titled "La cartuja" (*O.C.*, I, p. 823).

In his early poetry, insects and small animals had appeared mainly as he reflected on man's yearnings for transcendence and, in his particular case as an artist, as he considered his longings for ideal beauty. Lorca now expands these contexts and includes also a concern for human relationships.

As a brief reminder, the play is about a young cockroach who is also a poet. He senses the existence of a different reality, a world of beauty he sees reflected in the stars and embodied in the flowers. The other cockroaches cannot understand him and accuse him of laziness. One day, a wounded, white butterfly is found near the cockroaches' nest. They all marvel at her beauty and the insect-poet, whose name is Curianito El Nene, falls in love with her. Once healed the butterfly rejects him.

She belongs to a different world and she must return to it. The manuscript ends where Curianito watches helplessly as the butterfly flies away. He dies, but the circumstances are unknown. Those who saw the play cannot recall the exact ending and it is assumed that he dies in a futile attempt to follow her in flight or from a broken heart.

The analogy with the world of man is established early in the play. Lorca sets out to confront two basic attitudes, the visionary and the pragmatic which stem from a consideration of the age-old conflict between spirit and matter. This dichotomy is poetically expressed by creating two worlds in apparent opposition: a heavenly one where sources of light such as the moon and the stars serve to portray man's ideals and aspirations, and a terrestial one, the day-to-day world of the flesh. The opening lines of the prologue quickly state the problem:

> Señores: La comedia que vais a escuchar es humilde e inquietante, comedia rota del que quiere arañar a la luna y se araña su corazón.
> (*O.C.*, II, p. 5)

The adjective "humilde" has two functions. First, it indicates that a "tono menor" will prevail throughout the play and, second, it describes the humble nature of its principal characters and underlines the message of the play. "Inquietante" reveals Lorca's purpose which is to sensitize. "Comedia rota" refers to the treatment, a mixture of burlesque and farse with purely lyrical and tragic components. The verb "querer" alerts the public to the presence of a will and establishes the human parallel. The moon, a heavenly body, will serve as symbol of the superior world of the spirit, of the realm of the ideal. The heart, a vital organ and emblem of the emotions, stands for a more immediate reality. The verb "arañar" is an early recognition that man is incapable of totally grasping the ideal and suggests, at the same time, that the quest can have dangerous consequences.

Because Curianito El Nene is not only an insect but also an artist, two levels of meaning are interwoven in the play. Lorca consciously fuses a consideration of a basic human problem, the dichotomy flesh and spirit, with a consideration of a problem peculiar to the artist, his constant quest for ideal beauty; an ambitious project for so short a play. The quest for transcendence on the human level and the quest for ideal beauty are expressed by the same recurring image: a continuous desire to reach the heavens. This image can also be found in the works written prior to the play. We believe the moon is chosen instead of the stars because of Lorca's commitment to an observed natural world as we shall explain later.

Huge blades of grass, plants and trees evidence the presence of water in this terrestial or sub-lunar world. Very early in the play water is associated with love, and we remember that love has been offered as the only solution to man's ills in the prologue. This association is found in "Mañana," another poem written in 1918, where water/love appears as a force vital to spiritual and to physical well-being. Lorca recognized the importance of love but at the time he was writing these poems he was especially concerned with the general indifference to the values of the spirit (a fact that can be easily ascertained by reading his correspondence of that year). He, therefore, tended to emphasize a type of universal love. He himself felt that he could identify with all things and that he loved all things (*O.C.*, II, p. 1034).

In *El maleficio,* however, water, which appears in the form of dew to conform to the insect world, appears to be a symbol of a type of sensual love that can be more readily identified with "eros" than with "philia." We read in the prologue:

> El amor pasaba de padres a hijos como una joya vieja y exquisita que recibiera el primer insecto de las manos de Dios. Con la misma tranquilidad y la certeza que el polen de las flores se entrega al viento, ellos gozaban del amor bajo la hierba húmeda. (*O.C.*, II, p. 5)

The presence of "polen" and the verbs "entregar" an "gozar" suggest the carnal nature of this love which is in no way condemned by Lorca who describes it as an exquisite jewel given by God.

It is not surprising, therefore, that when Sylvia, a young cockroach who is hopelessly in love with Curianito, has to voice her frustrations she does so by complaining of thirst:

> Mis pesares son tan hondos
> como la laguna aquella
> (Con angustia)
> ¿Dónde está el agua
> tranquila y fresca
> que calme
> mi sed inquieta? (*O.C.*, II, p. 16)

Being an adolescent, she longs for the tranquil waters of the first love. She has yet to discover her sensuality like Belisa of *Don Perlimplín* or to experience the dark rivers of passion which later threaten the Novia in *Bodas de Sangre*.

Dew is, therefore, important in this insect world which is also inhabited by privileged creatures who, because they possess wings, can aspire to reach the heavens. In a poem written also in 1918 and which is believed to be a source for this play, a snail leaves his home in search for answers to the mysteries of life. He meets an ant who is being accused of being lazy. Her sole defense is that she has seen the stars and the experience has transformed her. She can only think and dream of them. Close to her death, she believes she hears the humming of a bee and assumes that it will take her to them. Wings, thus, play an important part in this early poetic world.

In *El maleficio,* the winged creature whose journey towards the heavens is interrupted, is a butterfly. She is white so she is probably a nocturnal one since most day butterflies are brightly colored. In English she would be called a moth. In a monologue the butterfly says that she is the spirit of the silk. At a purely anecdotical level we could assume that she is the moth of the silkworm which is also white. I have been told that Spanish children kept silkworms in boxes at home much like we keep gerbils or hamsters. I do not know if they still do. Lorca could have watched these creatures too but, in any event, all larvae spin cocoons with some type of fiber that he could have poetically identified with silk. It is known that these nocturnal creatures are attracted by sources of light and that one type in particular has a fixation for moonlight. In the play, the cockroaches actually bring the butterfly out into the open field so that the moonbeams may revive her. In an article on the Capek brothers and Lorca, Vera Beck-Agular[8] wonders whether Lorca knew the works of the entomologist J. H. Fabre who died in 1915 and whose works *La vie des Insects,* and *Souvenirs Entomologiques,* prompted several theatrical productions. Lorca's biographers make no mention of this but we do know that Lorca was a keen observer of nature and was undoubtedly aware of this phenomenon. Therefore, the moon was a more logical choice as representative of the heavens if he was to keep true to nature.

As a whole, there is very little action in the play. Its two acts are devoted mainly to a verbal confrontation by means of which the two sets of values and the two basic attitudes are constantly juxtaposed. Other structural devices contribute to this dramatic contrast and give the play a definite binary thrust. For example, the characters are aligned within a given attitude and even their language betrays their allegiance.

The process of metamorphosis is brought in to elaborate further the dichotomy spirit/matter and to introduce a discussion on the nature of love. In a monologue the butterfly says:

> Hilé mi corazón sobre carne
> para rezar en las tinieblas
> y la muerte me dio dos alas blancas
> pero cegó la fuente de mi seda.
>   . . .
> Ahora comprendo el lamentar del agua
> y el lamentar de las estrellas
> y el lamentar del viento en la montaña
> y el zumbido punzante
> de la abeja (*O.C.,* II, p. 45)

The symbolism is transparent. What was previously a crawling creature now, with wings, commands a different perspective. She understands the voices of nature; she is capable of a type of discernment which was earlier unknown to her. She realizes that something binds all creatures and that all of them yearn for the same thing. The transformation, however, has exacted a price.

To elaborate on this, Lorca introduces new characters quite late in the play. They are glowworms. Again Lorca makes use of another important symbol found in his early poetry: light. These creatures shed a type of earthly light that stands in contrast with the light of the heavenly bodies. They seem to be case in the role of philosophers since they ponder about the mysterious origins of the drops of dew and they reflect upon the fact that they are so fragile. One of them says:

> Gusano 3 — Los viejos
> sabemos que el amor
> es igual que el rocío.
> La gota que tú tragas
> no vuelve sobre el prado;
> como el amor, se pierde
> en la paz del olvido.

We cannot elaborate fully on Lorca's treatment of the theme of love in this play, but the idea expressed by the glowworms is that if love succumbs to time like dew, it should be enjoyed while there is life. Love is limited by time, therefore suggesting a physical or carnal type of love. The glowworms invite the butterfly to join them in their search for dew (love), but she surprises them by revealing that she has no mouth. She cannot drink the dew nor kiss, yet she has heard the drops of dew speak. This baffles the glowworms and suggests a different aspect of love. The verses in the butterfly's monologue, "la muerte de dio dos alas blancas pero cegó la fuente de mi seda," imply that the purely spiritual is barred from enjoying physical pleasures. The idea is introduced but the dilemma remains unresolved. The confrontation between the glowworms and the butterfly ends and the scene closes appropriately with a question.

If the butterfly stands for the spiritual, at the oppostie side we find the scorpion, el Alacranito Corta-Mimbres. This dangerous creature has been cast in the role of the "gracioso" by critics and it is true that he brings momentum to an otherwise static play. However, we are to keep in mind that Lorca has chosen a child-like perspective to deal with serious topics. Alacranito is the only one, of all the creatures, who cannot see beauty in the butterfly. He sees her merely as something edible. Alacranito is a drunkard and a bully whose only preoccupation is to satisfy his appetite. We believe that he stands in direct opposition to the butterfly whom he would gladly devour; he is a symbol of the purely instinctual which is portrayed early as a disruptive force that introduces violence and threatens death.

Curianito does declare his love to the butterfly and she rejects him. He dies. Lorca, up to this point, had been limiting himself to presenting the two sides of the human dilemma. However, the insect dies and his burial is solemn. Is he a victim of society or a victim of his artistic nature? The disturbing fact is that death seems to be the only solution offered, a tragic stance from the beginning and one which makes the more relevant and urgent the initial appeal, the call to be humble and to love.

It is known that Lorca moves on from this first pensive and reflexive stage into a more dynamic one. The preoccupation with matters of transcendence soon gives way to problems of self-realization. The new images adopted continue to follow a logic found in the natural world. The insects are not totally abandoned. They reappear when Lorca is again confronted with human need, with a break in human relationships and with an artificial way of life. This time it is in the city of New York where the long-contained rage of the outcasts dissolves butterflies in the window panes, butterflies that are, nevertheless, found nestled in the beard of Walt Whitman. The vision of the heavens has clearly weakened as the vision of life has become more tragic. In *Poeta en Nueva York* we read:

> Existen las montañas, lo sé.
> y los anteojos para la sabiduría,
> lo sé. Pero yo no he venido a ver el cielo.
> He venido para ver la turbia sangre,
> la sangre que lleva las máquinas a las cataratas
> y el espíritu a la lengua de la cobra.
> (*O.C.*, I, p. 517)

There are sentiments, in both his mature poetry and mature plays, that are best understood if we have a knowledge of this early poetic world and the context which guided the poet.

Ruth Ayéndez-Alder
North Carolina State University

NOTES

[1] See, for example, Carlos Ramos-Gil, *Claves Líricas de García Lorca* (Madrid: Aguilar, S.A., 1964), p. 25.

[2] Federico García Lorca, *Obras Completas,* I and II (Madrid: Aguilar, S.A., 1974). Quotes will be indicated within the text with a Roman numeral for the volume and an Arabic one for the page.

[3] Francisco García Lorca, Prologue to *Three Tragedies of Federico García Lorca* (New York: New Directions, 1947), p. 7.

[4] José Luis Cano, *García Lorca, Biografía ilustrada* (Barcelona: Ediciones Destino, 1969), p. 44.

[5] Rafael Altamir Erevea, *Arte y Realidad* (Cataluña: Editorial Cervantes, 1921), pp. 157-160.

[6] José Mora Guarnido, *Ferderico García Lorca y su mundo* (Buenos Aires: Editorial Losada, S.A., 1958), p. 125.

[7] Alfredo de la Guardia, *García Lorca, persona y creación* (Buenos Aires: Editorial Schapire, 1965), p. 261.

[8] Vera F. de Beck-Agular, "Entomological symbols in the Capeks and García Lorca," *Literature East and West,* 9 (1965), p. 101.

DOORS AND WINDOWS AS A LURING CALL OF NATURE IN THE WORK OF FEDERICO GARCÍA LORCA

> "Throw wide open your doors and windows,
> you girls who live in the town.
> The reaper asks you for roses
> with which to deck his crown."
> Federico García Lorca, *The House of Bernarda Alba*

Federico García Lorca, speaking about Fuente Vaqueros, his birthplace near Granada, once said: "My whole childhood is a village with shepherds, fields, sky, solitude. In one word: simplicity. I am greatly surprised when people see in my writings the daring tricks and audacity of a poet. They are not. They are authentic accounts that many believe unusual because it is also unusual to approach life in such a rare and simple way: by seeing and listening."[1]

It was in Fuente Vaqueros that Federico made his first encounter with nature when as a little boy he would spend hours conversing with insects and animals and sing with the running water that sprang forth from the fountain and with the wind in the trees. Nature was every day's reality as he accompanied through the fields his father who was a gentleman farmer. For him every particle of nature had a soul, and one afternoon, as he was walking in his parents' patio, he suddenly heard someone spelling out his name: Fe-de-ri-co! He looked around and saw no one. And then, he realized it was the old poplar tree that was singing aloud his name as the wind moved through its leaves.

Federico García Lorca was never to close the door to the magic world of his childhood. That childhood remained alive in him without ever becoming a recollection. He kept wide open that door to his infancy to let the magic spell of his childhood flow over into his adulthood. And his work, be it prose or poetry (and Lorca permeated poetry even in his plays), is a continuous dialogue with every element of nature.

To Lorca the poet is a medium who can establish a receptive contact with nature because he has drawn open all the doors of communication with the senses to enter into the realm of the unknown, without ever losing touch with reality, that firsthand knowledge from which stems his poetic creation:

> The poet is a medium
> of Nature
> who explains its greatness
> by means of words.
>
> The poet understands
> the incomprehensible
> and he holds as his friends
> things that others hate.[2]

"The poet," he says "is a tree"[3] and "trees are arrows from heaven."[4] The poet therefore is the best commentator of heaven and earth. He can talk to the stars and he can learn the hidden secrets of the fountain. "Who taught you the way to poetry?" ask of him some children in the poem "The Ballad of the Small Village Square," and he answers: "The fountain and the brook of the ancient song."[5]

It is then more than logical that nature would become the symbol of life with all its primitive impulses and instincts and that the women characters in his plays would dream of a lover by the seashore or in the midst of the meadow. Water is perhaps the element that he uses the most in his plays, because his characters suffer from repression and seek water to quench their thirst, be it in the form of a glass of water, dewdrops, rain, a well, a brook, a river, the ocean. "I want to get married to a beautiful manly man from the shore of the sea,"[6] says María Josefa, the eighty year old grandmother in *The House of Bernarda Alba* as she dreams of freedom and cries out: "Let me out,"[7] "You are going to open the door for me?"[8] She holds in her arms a little lamb as if he were her baby, for as she so justly says: "It's better to have a lamb than not to have anything,"[9] and she goes on singing:

> Little lamb, child of mine,
> Let's go to the shore of the sea,
> The tiny ant will be at his doorway,
> I'll nurse you and give you your bread.[10]

Doors and windows are therefore used in Lorca's plays as a way of escaping into the liberating forces of nature, and nature for his women characters are representative of man and fulfillment in him. Belisa, in *Don Perlimplín and Belisa,* opens the curtains of her balcony and almost naked sings languidly of love. Adela, in *The House of Bernarda Alba,* stands at night by her window with wrought-iron bars with the light shining on her half-naked body to wait for her man, Pepe the Roman, who is as dynamic to her as the wild stallions to the mare. "My body will be for whomever I choose,"[11] she says defiantly. On her wedding night, Belisa leaves open the five balconies through which the white light of dawn and the wind enter to let in the sweet scent of the garden. And it will be in that same garden that she falls in love with an unknown gallant who is none other than her own husband in disguise:

> Upon the banks of the river
> the passing night has paused to bathe.
> . . . .
> And on the breasts of Belisa
> the flowers languish of their love.[12]

The shoemaker's wife, in *The Shoemaker's Prodigious Wife,* dreams of a lover riding a black mare covered with tassels and little mirrors and is irritated by the commonplace appearance of her own husband. However, when her husband leaves her, she unconsciously adorns him with the qualities that she would have wanted him to possess and she pictures their love by the side of a brook: "When I met him I was washing clothes in the little brook. Through half a yard of water the pebbles on the bottom could be seen laughing—laughing with little tremblings. He wore a tight black suit, a red tie of the finest silk, and four gold rings that shone like four suns."[13] When she does not go herself into the make-believe world of fantasy, the spirit of fantasy comes to visit her in the form of a multicolored butterfly as it enters through her window. The butterfly and the young boy who runs after it are symbols of the happiness and freedom that she was never given to enjoy and for a moment she feels fulfilled: as she is taken into the magic world of nature:

> Butterfly of the breezes,
> wind-creature so lovely;
> butterfly of the breezes
> so green, so golden,
> a candle's flame;
> butterfly of the breezes,
> I beg you, stay here, stay here, stay here!
> I beg you, stay here!
> Butterfly, oh, please, are you here?[14]

Lorca draws a distinctive demarcation line between the freedom of the outside world that filters through the iron bolts of the doors and the bars of the windows and the world within the confinement of doors and windows. Outside there is life and laughter; inside envy and bitterness; outside there are men singing as they work in the fields; inside there are women locked up in a suffocating atmosphere. "I can't be locked up. I don't want my skin to look like yours. I don't want skin's whiteness lost in these rooms. Tomorrow I'm going to put on my green dress and go walking in the streets. I want to go out,"[15] says Adela in *The House of Bernarda Alba* and she adds: "How I'd like to be a reaper so I could come and go as I please."[16] Her sister Amelia answers: "To be born a woman is the worst possible punishment."[17] And they long for freedom and for love within the soothing elements of nature:

> The reapers have set out
> Looking for ripe wheat.
> They'll carry off the hearts
> Of any girl they meet.[18]

What is the house of Bernarda Alba but a fortress or medieval convent with thick white walls and windows with bars that imprison the women characters in a stifling, devouring atmosphere. Bernarda, the authoritarian mother, rules over her household with the strict order of living as if the doors and windows were sealed with bricks. But the five daughters and their grandmother rebel in a defiant struggle for survival. For that reason the door to the corral and the windows take on for them an unusual proportion, as if nothing else existed. They represent their freedom, the outside world which comes to them in the form of the wind or a breeze, the scent of flowers, the handsome figure of a man. Their thirst for life makes them want to draw open all the doors and all the windows to appease the scorching fire that ignites them. María Josefa, the grandmother, says: "Now I have to go away, but I'm afraid the dogs will bite me. Won't you come with me as far as the fields? I want fields, I want houses, but open houses, and the neighbor women asleep in their beds with their tiny tots, and the men outside sitting in their chairs."[19] Martirio repeats the song of the reapers, which is symbolic of the five sisters' repressed desire for love:

> Throw wide open your doors and windows,
> You girls who live in town.[20]

Federico García Lorca communicates as easily with people as with insects, animals, the tingling water, or a star. His characters may well be a man, a woman, a child, a butterfly. Indeed, nature is often the real protagonist, for if after seeing a play we are struck by the forcefulness of its characters, we are also responding to the vibrant call of the Andalusian countryside.

Lorca the child, the man, and the poet loved the earth with all its subtleties. Nature was every day's reality which he transfigured into the magic of his poetry. "I love the earth," he once said. "I feel bound to it in all my emotions. My most remote childhood memories have a taste of earth. The earth, the fields have brought great things into my life. Insects of the earth, animals, and peasants suggest things that few people can understand. I grasp them now with the same spirit as in my childhood years."[21]

It is of no surprise then that as a poet Lorca would play with doors and windows to lure his characters to the triumphant world of nature. The thick walls of frustration are pushed away, the doors and windows are thrown wide open to let the exuberant spell of nature take over. Lorca shares this spell with all of us as he says: "Until you learn to love deeply the stones and the caterpillars, you will not enter the Kingdom of Heaven. ... The Kingdom of plants and animals is near at hand; though Man forgets his Maker, plants and animals are very near the light. And,

Poet, tell men that love is born with the same exaltation in all planes of life—that the rhythm of a leaf swaying in the wind is the same as that of a distant star, and that the very words spoken by the fountain in the shade are repeated by the sea, and in the same tone. Tell Man to be humble. In nature, all things are equal."[22]

Marie-Lise Gazarian-Gautier
St. John's University

NOTES

[1] Federico García Lorca, *Obras completas* (Madrid: Aguilar, 1967), pp. 1770-1771.

[2] Federico García Lorca, "Este es el prólogo," *Obras completas*, pp. 583-584.

[3] Federico García Lorca, *Ibid.*, p. 583.

[4] Federico García Lorca, "Arboles," *Obras completas*, p. 264.

[5] Federico García Lorca, "Balada de la placeta," *Obras completas*, p. 251.

[6] Federico García Lorca, *The House of Bernarda Alba*, in *Three Tragedies* (New York: New Directions Book, 1947), p. 175.

[7] Federico García Lorca, *Ibid.*, p. 165.

[8] Federico García Lorca, *Ibid.*, p. 206.

[9] Federico García Lorca, *Ibid.*

[10] Federico García Lorca, *Ibid.*, p. 207.

[11] Federico García Lorca, *Ibid.*, p. 181.

[12] Federico García Lorca, *The Love of Don Perlimplín and Belisa in the Garden*, in *Five Plays by Lorca* (New York: New Directions Book, 1963), p. 126.

[13] Federico García Lorca, *The Shoemaker's Prodigious Wife*, in *Five Plays by Lorca*, p. 84.

[14] Federico García Lorca, *Ibid.*, pp. 77-78.

[15] Federico García Lorca, *The House of Bernarda Alba*, in *Three Tragedies*, p. 173.

[16] Federico García Lorca, *Ibid.*, p. 185.

[17] Federico García Lorca, *Ibid.*

[18] Federico García Lorca, *Ibid.*

[19] Federico García Lorca, *Ibid.*, p. 206.

[20] Federico García Lorca, *Ibid.*, p. 186.

[21] Federico García Lorca, *Obras completas*, p. 1754.

[22] Federico García Lorca, *The Butterfly's Evil Spell*, in *Five Plays by Lorca*, p. 194.

NATURE'S SENSUAL AND SEXUAL ASPECTS IN THREE GYPSY BALLADS OF GARCÍA LORCA

In his *Romancero gitano,* Federico García Lorca constructs a perfect assimilation of form and content. The form is, of course, that of the traditional *romance,* complete with its *fragmentismo*[1] or enigmatic open-endedness which excites the reader's imagination and makes him an accomplice to the poetic process. The content reflects the primitive popular world of the gypsies as perceived through the civilized, yet creative eye of a poet sympathetic to their plight, which Honig describes as "the sorrows of a persecuted people living on the margins of society, who maintain their old tribal primitivism intact."[2] In a similar vein, Mora Guarnido explains the persecution suffered by the gypsy as a result of his life style, indifferent and scornful of "lo castellano," and "su resistencia al mestizaje y su condición trashumante que le hace considerar toda permanencia en la tierra como provisional."[3]

The three *romances* which I have chosen for this study fall into the category which Díaz-Plaja calls that of "las fuerzas oscuras"[4] and are permeated by the forces of nature. This poetic world is a wealth of metaphors of sensuality and sexuality through which nature interacts directly with the human psyche or stands aside to observe the human condition with an attitude ranging from sympathetic, to indifferent, to openly antagonistic. "Romance sonámbulo," "Romance de la luna, luna," and "Preciosa y el aire" form a kind of trilogy, profane trinity or triangle. At the two base angles of this triangle we can place "Preciosa y el aire" and "Romance de la luna, luna," respectively. In both works an element of nature is personified to assume a powerful sexual role, in one case feminine and in the other masculine, while the rest of nature looks on with ambivalence. "Romance sonámbulo" constitutes the apex of the triangle where nature embodies cosmic, omnipotent sexuality and keeps an ironic vigil over a pathetic human reality of frustrated love and death.

Consonant with the spirit of gypsy superstition, "Romance de la luna, luna"[5] portrays the moon as a woman—a femme fatale, a seductress—both attractive and repelling. In spite of her blatant sexual overtures, her obscene undulating dance intended to bewitch and mesmerize the gypsy boy, Lorca also depicts her as something of a prude with innate frigidity that is made apparent in both visual and tactile metaphors of her coldness and whiteness. Thus the moon, in spite of feminine frills like her "polisón de nardos," has "senos de duro estaño" and speaks of preserving her "blancor almidonado." The boy even admonishes her that if captured, the gypsies will make of her unfeeling heart "collares y anillos blancos." She is perhaps the eternal tease, taunting and tantalizing, yet ultimately untouchable, the virgin whose pleasure lies in the conquest without carnal consummation. The human emotion of love does not exist here. The attraction that radiates from the moon is purely sexual; there is nothing tender in her advances.

Lorca suddenly changes scenes and describes the return of the gypsies. The two verses during which we are absent from the force provide enough time for the moon to have worked her mysterious magic and when we return, "el niño tiene los ojos cerrados." On one plane of reality, the child is dead, mourned by the tears and cries of the gypsies. With awareness but indifference to human grief, nature again appears in the final verses, somewhat as it will in the "Romance sonámbulo." Lorca now refers to the air, which engulfs and fuses us to the rest of the natural world, and which is simply watching: "El aire la vela, vela./El aire la está velando." The strange appearance of the moon cannot be explained away rationally as a fantasy of the *niño* or as a purely poetic device to describe his death. The moon's mystery and her successful seduction are continued in a verse of tremendous visual impact: "Por el cielo va la luna/con un niño de la mano."

The moon, so often utilized by Lorca to symbolize sensuality and death, as does the color green, appears in this poem to synthesize perfectly her paradoxical poetic value. She is both seducer and harbinger of death, not unlike her role in *Bodas de sangre* where, jealous of the men's passion for a woman, she illuminates the rivals so that their knives can find their marks. It is as if her cold whiteness thrived on the warmth and passion of human blood. In *Bodas de sangre* she says: "¡no podrán escaparse!", "¡Tengo frío!", "¡Que quiero entrar en un pecho/para poder calentarme!", "Pero que tarden mucho en morir. Que la sangre/me ponga entre los dedos su delicado silbo."[6] In "Romance sonámbulo"[7] death's cold victory over human love once again can be inferred from the chilling visual image of the moon reflecting the body of the gypsy girl in the cistern: "Un carámbano de luna/la sostiene sobre el agua."

"Preciosa y el aire"[8] views the gypsy world both in its relationship to nature and as a marginal reality living on the fringes of established bourgeois society. Whereas in "Romance de la luna, luna" the moon appears as a female force in the symbolic seduction of a *gitanito,* here the wind is portrayed as a ravaging, savage *macho,* determined to violate the gypsy girl. The air, which is depicted as conscious but static in "Romance de la luna, luna," becomes "el viento que nunca duerme," "sátiro," "San Cristobalón desnudo," all of which allude to dynamic and purposeful motion. Pagan mythology, Christian symbolism and primitive superstition are synthesized in this wind who is at once Pan, St. Christopher and the breath of life. The *romance* begins by evoking the music played by Preciosa on her tambourine or "luna de pergamino." In an atmosphere of sylvan revelry, the rhythm acquires hypnotic power over her, lowering the threshold of her conscious self so that she becomes an integral part of her surroundings, drawn into the web of nature.[9] Thus stripped of the trappings of consciousness, she excites the raw virility of the wind, "viento-hombrón," "viento verde," which rises to penetrate her innocent purity. If the images describing the moon emphasized her frigidity, the wind's searing passion is described with obvious phallic symbols such as "espada caliente" and "lenguas relucientes." He says to the *gitana:*

> Niña, deja que levante
> tu vestido para verte.
> Abre en mis dedos antiguos
> la rosa azul de tu vientre.

Unlike the antagonistic attitude of nature contained in "Romance sonámbulo," here there is concern, even alarm, expressed by the part of nature which observes the wind's attack:

> Frunce su rumor el mar.
> Los olivos palidecen.
> ....
> ¡Preciosa, corre, Preciosa!
> ¡Míralo por donde viene!

Although the girl at least provisionally escapes the clutches of the wind, her refuge ironically underlines the gypsies' state as social outcasts, spurned by conventional society while trying to maintain their unique cultural heritage. She flees to the house of the English consul where she is surrounded by curious *carabineros* and is offered a "copa de ginebra" which she significantly does not drink. The pristine sensuality of her encounter with nature is contrasted in this scene with the trite, stuffy and artificial world of the bourgeoisie. But Lorca does not permit this world to overcome the force of nature. We are not allowed to dismiss the sexual advances of the wind as merely a fantasy conjured up by the girl's imagination and sensibility to nature. Just as in "Romance de la luna, luna," another powerful visual image sustains the poetic plane: "en las tejas de pizarra/el viento, furioso, muerde."

"Romance sonámbulo," at the apex of the triangle analogy, is a poem whose beauty lies in the richness of its dreamlike images and the very rhythm of the language. Here no particular element of nature is singled out for a sexual role to interplay with human reality, but the color *verde,* nature's predominant color, permeates the work on all levels. Lorca's use of the full range of this color's suggestive quality establishes the ambiguous atmosphere of this ballad. The repetition of the refrain, "Verde que te quiero verde,/Verde viento. Verdes ramas.," evinces green in its most typical imagery—that of nature's sensual fulfillment: spring, rebirth and hope. Green also manifests itself paradoxically through tragic implications of death, although there is coherency if one views death as a reintegration into nature. The gypsy girl who once awaited the return of her lover with "cara fresca, negro pelo," now awaits him motionless in death[10] with "verde carne, pelo verde," and unseeing eyes "de fría plata." The static description of her is counterpoised by the dynamics of nature: "las cosas la están mirando/y ella no puede mirarlas."

All of the imagery employed in this poem to paint a back drop of a hostile nature which bears witness to human tragedy appeals to the senses. Creating the sensation of cold, there are "grandes estrellas de escarcha" and "un carámbano de luna." We are made to taste the wind, "un raro gusto/de hiel, de menta y de albahaca." Sound, touch and sight are stimulated by metaphors of the world's self-assertion in "the spasmodic clash of its forms:"[11]

> La higuera frota su viento
> con la lija de sus ramas,
> y el monte, gato garduño,
> eriza sus pitas agrias.
> . . . .
> Mil panderos de cristal,
> herían la madrugada.

The menacing movements of nature are not the only actions in the poem. This activity has a human parallel introduced by the question "¿Pero quién vendrá? ¿Y por dónde. . .?" The girl's gypsy lover has returned, only to be confronted with her death, so poignantly lamented by her father in the couplet "Pero yo ya no soy yo,/ni mi casa es ya mi casa." But the young man as well is in the process of losing his vitality, running down like an unwound clock, approaching the static state of death, "dejando un rastro de sangre." His wound, although left unexplained as is the girl's death, brings to mind the conflict between the gypsies and the unsympathetic outside world. Its fatality is portended metaphorically as "trescientas rosas morenas," brown not red, just as the girl's hair is no longer black but green. It is only at the end of the poem that nature relents and shows compassion harmonious with the tragedy. For a fleeting instant, this empathy is felt in the line: "La noche se puso íntima/como una pequeña plaza." But just as quickly, another hostile force is introduced, this one from the world of men, jolting and destroying the tragic though tranquil scene of intimacy: "Guardias civiles borrachos/en la puerta golpeaban."

Although nature functions in this poem chiefly as an impassive observer to human death and grief, its latent sexuality deserves further mention. In the refrain,

> Verde que te quiero verde.
> Verde viento. Verdes ramas.
> El barco sobre la mar.
> Y el caballo en la montaña.

I have interpreted green as the color of the sensuality and procreation of nature. This interpretation is heightened by the linguistic device of juxtaposing masculine and feminine nouns in a sort of permanent telluric intercourse: "viento" and "ramas," "*el* barco sobre *la* mar," and "*el* caballo en *la* montaña." This same linguistic technique can be found in the words of the *mocito* who begs to exchange his life of dangerous adventure for a more domestic existence beside his beloved. The meaning and gender of the nouns juxtaposed produce a similar effect:

> Compadre, quiero cambiar
> mi caballo par su casa,
> mi montura por su espejo,
> mi cuchillo por su manta.

But the possibilities of human love are frustrated and unattainable. While nature, both sensual and hostile, looks on mockingly, the established social order in the form of the Civil Guard deals the final crushing blow.

Thus in these three poems lie three different, yet kindred portrayals of nature and its interrelation with human life. In "Romance de la luna, luna," the moon seduces and kidnaps a gypsy boy resulting in his death, at least on the first level of reality. In "Preciosa y el aire," the howling wind is intent on violating the *gitana*, who escapes his lust by fleeing to the security of an alien culture, perhaps equally threatening to her integrity as gypsy as the wind was to her virginity. And in the "Romance sonámbulo," nature is a sexually prepotent ironic observer to the tragedy of death and unfulfilled young love:

> ¡Cuántas veces te esperó!
> ¡Cuántas veces te esperara,
> cara fresca, negro pelo,
> en esta verde baranda!

In spite of apparent paradoxes in Lorca's use of natural

imagery, there is coherency in his metaphoric system if one is willing to accept the contradictions of life itself. If the moon can be personified as a cold and calculating temptress, why should the wind not become a lascivious male in hot pursuit of his prey? And if green can be used to suggest hope and rebirth, why should it not also be used to represent death and despair?, opposites, yes, but inconceivable without each other. In explaining the origin of the poetic image, Lorca once stated: "La metáfora une dos mundos antagónicos por medio de un salto ecuestre que da la imaginación."[12] We, his readers, must be willing to accompany him on this flight of the imagination. But even then, as in all great literature, each rereading, each successive leap, offers new interpretations revealing the unfathomable genious of his inspiration, his *duende*.

Bonnie Shannon McSorley
Northeastern University

NOTES

[1] C. Colin Smith, "Introduction," *Spanish Ballads,* ed. Smith (Oxford: Pergamon Press, 1964), p. 30.

[2] Edwin Honig, "Triumph of Sensual Reality—Mature Verse," in *Lorca: A Collection of Critical Essays,* ed. Manuel Durán (Englewood Cliffs: Prentice Hall, 1965), p. 80.

[3] José Mora Guarnido, *Federico García Lorca y su mundo* (Buenos Aires: Losada, 1958), p. 188.

[4] Guillermo Díaz-Plaja, *Federico García Lorca* (Madrid: Espasa Calpe, 1961), p. 124.

[5] *Obras completas* (Madrid: Aguilar, 1966), pp. 425-26. Hereafter cited as *Obras.*

[6] *Obras,* pp. 1249-51.

[7] *Obras,* pp. 430-32.

[8] *Obras,* pp. 426-28.

[9] See Rupert C. Allen, *The Symbolic World of Federico García Lorca* (Albuquerque: University of New Mexico Press, 1972), pp. 15-33 for a detailed study of collective, individual and reduced consciousness.

[10] I interpret her as dead, perhaps because of her heart-breaking vigil, and reflected in the cistern by the moonlight. Some other critics will not agree. Arturo Barea, for example, sees her as having drowned as a result of her sleepwalking in *Lorca: The Poet and His People* (New York: Harcourt, Brace, 1949), p. 128. J. B. Hall implies that she has intentionally committed suicide by drowning herself in "Lorca's *Romancero gitano,*" in *Studies of the Spanish and Portuguese Ballad,* ed. N. D. Shergold (London: Tamesis, 1972), p. 152. Howard T. Young explains her immobility as a

dreamlike state of enchantment or trance in *The Victorious Expression: A Study of Four Contemporary Spanish Poets* (Madison: University of Wisconsin Press: 1966), p. 173. For Rupert Allen, she is an adulterous wife, murdered by her husband, "An Analysis of Narrative and Symbol in Lorca's 'Romance sonámbulo'," *Hispanic Review*, 36 (1968), pp. 342-43.

[11]Juan López-Morillas, "Lyrical Primitivism: García Lorca's *Romancero gitano*," in *Lorca: A Collection of Critical Essays*, p. 136.

[12]"La imagen poética de don Luis de Góngora," in *Obras*, p. 69.

THE MYTHICAL ASPECT OF DEATH IN THE NATURAL WORLD OF THE *ROMANCERO GITANO*

One of Lorca's purposes in writing the *Romancero gitano* was to create and perpetuate the myth of the Andalusian gypsy. Since a hostile environment is intrinsic to any mythology, it is not surprising that the world of nature depicted in the poems is a constant threat to human existence. The most extreme manifestation of nature's malevolence in the *Romancero gitano* is, of course, that of death, which is omnipresent and can strike at any time from any place. Thus, its agent may be a cosmic force ("Romance de la luna, luna"); other gypsies, whether one man is killed ("Muerte de Antoñito el Camborio") or many ("Reyerta"); or an unspecified, mysterious cause about which the reader is free to specullate ("Romance sonámbulo").

This study concentrates on the mythological background of certain animal symbols that connote death in the *Romancero gitano*. It proposes to show how Lorca, to reinforce the mythical quality of his work, selected the symbols from traditional mythological (and at times religious or folkloric) sources. Hopefully, the discussion will also indicate his artistry in incorporating them into his narratives, and explain how the combination of selectivity and poetic skill support the criticism that the *Romancero gitano* is the poet's most successful and most representative collection of poems.[1] The limitation of time dictates that the detailed analyses required here be restricted to three favorite animals from Lorca's world of nature. They are, in order of presentation, the dog, the dove, and the fabled unicorn.

The subject of "Muerto de amor" is an intense, bloody gypsy feud that takes place as "La noche llama temblando/al cristal de los balcones,/perseguida por los mil/perros que no la conocen." The reference to the dog(s) recalls the power, destructive force and relationship with death that many ancient civilizations attributed to the animal. Four associations with life giving, life taking deities especially exemplify the dog's potency. It was the symbol of both the Semitic healing and protecting mother goddess Gula, and of Hecate, the Greek goddess of the moon, earth and underworld. Marduk, god of the sun and war in the Babylonian-Assyrian pantheon, was represented as four dogs. And the Hindu Shiva, symbol of the creative and destructive forces of nature, appeared as a black dog, astride a dog.

The correspondence between the animal and death in "Muerto de amor" reflects the ancients' view that the dog was a psychopomp, or a direct or indirect cause of death. Like the vulture it accompanied the dead on their nocturanl trip by sea to the realm beyond the tomb. Amratians buried the dog with its master to guide him to the next world; and Anubis, the Egyptian dog-headed messenger of the gods, conducted souls to the promised land. Yudhishthira, hero of the Indian epic *Mahabharata*, refused to enter heaven without his dog. Greek mythology offers many examples of the relationship between dog and death. Oenus was killed for throwing stones at a dog, and Pindareus for stealing a golden dog. Crotopus's dogs devoured Linus, King Aidoneous flung Peirithous to the two-headed Cerberus; and the monster Scylla, which devoured some of Odysseus's crew, had six dogs for legs. Acteon's grieving hound exemplified the universal association between a howling dog and death. In the cosmos Canis Minor and Sirius, the Dog Star, were agents of drought and famine.

The Judaeo-Christian tradition maintained the negative aspect of the dog.[2] Haranians, whose priests engaged in sodomy, burned live dogs in sacrifices. Hebrews abominated the animal as a ceremoniously unclean scavenger. The Old Testament associates dogs with the devouring of dead bodies (I Kings 14:11; 21:19, 23, 24; 22:38), applies the word dog as a term of self-reproach or humility (I Samuel 24:14; II Samuel 3:8, 9:8, 16:9; II Kings 8:13), and uses it metaphorically as a synonym for sinner, pariah or cruel enemy (Psalms 22:16, 20). The animal fared little better in the Christian era. The Middle Ages established the dog as the Devil, the hound of hell. Stan appeared to St. Dunstan and St. Waltheof as a dog, and the animal was seen in the company of witches and agents of the Devil. The baying dog meant imminent death, and to meet a black dog presaged certain death.

Lorca's poem, therefore, continues a tradition that emanated in primitive civilizations, became a part of Classical mythology, reinforced itself in the Middle Ages, and formed an important part of the gypsy heritage. The dog as a symbol of fidelity, "man's best friend," is irrelevant in the *Romancero gitano*. Its relationship with death in "Muerto de amor" calls upon the negative aspect, long entrenched in many civilizations. Especially interesting is the correspondence between dogs and dawn in the poem. Based on primitive belief, dawn is the time of the eternal battle in Lorca's poetry, when night and day compete for supremacy, as winter and spring, and life and death, do in their own time. In "Muerto de amor" the gypsy feud is the timeless struggle, and the dog again is an integral part of it. Lorca recognized the importance of the belief in Egypt, long assumed to be the ancestral home of the gypsies. He artistically incorporated that primitive trait into the gypsy world of his time to stress the continuity of life and thought throughout their development. The correspondence between the dog and death, drawn from several mythologies, logically fits into the ballad and stresses the mythological nature of the *Romancero gitano*.

The historical ballad, "Thamar y Amnón," highlights the story of incest between King David's children from II Samuel 13. Both versions tell of the princess's beauty, Amnon's deception, the rape, and the resultant heartbreak in David's household. But whereas Lorca ends his poem with the sad king's cutting the strings of his harp, the Old Testament continues through Absolom's revenge, the command to kill his treacherous half-brother, and his flight to Geshur after its fulfillment.

Tamar is introduced in the poem, ". . .cantando/desnuda por la terraza./Alrededor de sus pies,/cinco palomas heladas." The source of the dove as a nefarious symbol is a myth that dates back to almost the traditional dawn of civilization. The inhabitants of the Fertile Crescent of Mesopotamia personified the soil as Ishtar, to whom they assigned the dove as a symbol of peace and productivity. Once Ishtar became a principal deity in Babylonia and Assyria, her worship spread to other lands under various names, among them Ashtaroth, Atargatis and Astarte. As the daughter of Anu she was the goddess of pure love and fertility; but as the daughter of Sin she became associated with lust, illicit love, and even with war and death. Sacred prostitution was practiced in her temples, and prostitutes considered her their patroness. The hero of the Babylonian Gilgamesh epic spurned her as a faithless woman and a murderer of former lovers. King Hammurabi referred to Ishtar as the "Lady of Battles," while statues represented her astride a lion, weapon in hand. The association of Ishtar with impure love and violence consequently increased the negative symbolism of the dove among the ancients.[3]

In time Ishtar's traits were transferred to the Greek Aphrodite, whose birth associated her with both the dove and violence. According to Hesiod she was born in the sea near Cythera of the foam and the blood of the castrated Uranus. Hyginus places her birth in the River Euphrates, where she emerged from an egg that had been hatched by doves. Like Ishtar, Aphrodite was the embodiment of pure and heavenly love (Aphrodite Urania) and of carnal love (Aphrodite Pandemos). Her involvements in acts of love ranged from questionable incidents at best to adultery and incest, the crime in "Thamar y Amnón." Because of the amorous goddess Helius fell in love with Leucothoë, causing the latter's death; and Paris abducted Helen, leading to the Trojan War. Her punishment of Calliope resulted in the death of Orpheus; and she caused Medea to love Jason, anticipating the betrayal of Medea's brother and father, Aeëtes. Aphrodite's own love affairs were with both mortals, such as Anchises, whom she crippled, and gods, the celebrated one being her lying with Ares during the absence of her husband Hephaestus. She compounded her own adultery with that of Tyndareus's daughters, whom she caused to be unfaithful to their husbands; and she forced incest upon Myrrha and Phaedra. Like Ishtar, she eventually became associated with prostitution; and her original pristine character degenerated into that of a mere patroness of prostitutes.

The frozen doves at Tamar's feet derive from the dove associated with Aphrodite. Lorca incorporated into the poem the various negative traits associated with the goddess—illicit love, violence and sadness—and pluralized the dove to form a correspondence with one of his prime symbols of death, the moon. That in turn is reinforced by other harbingers of tragedy such as "metal," "panderos fríos," "copos," "granizo" and "puñales," white or gray in color, cold to the senses. All appear in the first part of the poem to suggest that Tamar is predestined to play a tragic role in the ballad, just as Aphrodite's birth from an act of violence foreshadowed her unfavorable role in mythology. Lorca did not intend to equate Tamar with Aphrodite, but to cast her as the innocent victim of incestuous love, transmitted from the Asiatic Ishtar through the Aphrodite Pandemos (and the Roman Venus, of course). The effects are as widespread in the ballad as they are in mythology. The violated Tamar is spiritually dead, David grieves of the domestic disgrace; and after the climax of Lorca's poem, Amnon will meet a violent end when, "the servants of Absolom did to Amnon as Absolom had commanded" (verse 29).

The "Burla de Don Pedro a caballo" is Lorca's version of the legend of Don Bueso, a French knight killed by Bernardo del Carpio. By the Golden Age Don Bueso, or Boyso (modern name, Pedro), had become a heroic figure of Spanish ballads; and Lope de Vega presented that quality in his *Caballero de Olmedo,* the protagonist of which is named Don Alonso. By the late sixteenth century Don Bueso had also become a comic figure, and Lorca's version exaggerates the character to the extreme by treating the theme as a *burla.* Like Lope he skillfully combines history and reality with artistry and fantasy, but he denies Don Pedro the heroism and dignity of the *comedia* and earlier versions. The protagonist here passes through a dreamlike atmosphere only to die in a pool of water, "jugando con las ranas."[4]

An important symbol in the poem is the "unicornio de ausencia," which "rompe en cristal su cuerno" upon Don Pedro's death. The unicorn, described by Ctesias in the fifth century B.C., was a puzzling animal that probably originated through confusion with the rhinoceros of India. To compound the problem, the Hebrew word "re'em" or wild ox, appeared in the Vulgate as "unicornis" or "rhinoceros" and in the King James version as "unicorn." Debate over its existence continued between scientists who discounted Pliny's description and explorers who claimed to have seen the unicorn in such remote areas as Tibet.[5]

But the unicorn did become a part of tradition, and one of its principal traits, swiftness, caused it to be portrayed as a hunted animal. The Unicorn Tapestries in the Cloisters in New York

City, for example, show a unicorn pursued by hunters, wild animals and hounds. On occasion, however, the unicorn was the hunter, usually symbolizing death. It represents death in pursuit of man in the "Allegory of Human Life" from the *Legend of Barlaam and Josaphat.* Death rides a unicorn in Jean Colombe's miniature in the *Hours of Chantilly,* and in Durer's *Rape of Persephone* the animal carries Pluto and his abducted bride to the Underworld.

Don Pedro's mad gallop at the beginning of Lorca's poem ("montado en un ágil/caballo sin freno") indicates that he may be, like the mythical unicorn, either the hunter ("venía en la busca/del pan y del beso") or the hunted, the intended victim, his role in legend and literature. The reader may interpret the protagonist's death as a type of "hunting accident" while he travels in haste through the night or assume that Don Pedro is murdered as in previous versions. Lorca intentionally keeps the circumstances as mysterious as the atmosphere that surrounds the events. If don Pedro is indeed the "hunted," it is not clear whether he is overcome by mortal or supernatural forces. The narrative is imprecise enough to obscure whether the ballad's principal motif, the moon, is an omen, the actual instrument of death, or whether Don Pedro merely merges symbolically with it upon his death.

Two time honored traits of the unicorn, its ability to cure and its nobility, reinforce Lorca's ironic treatment of the Don Bueso legend. Many persons, among them the authority Aelian, perceived the animal's "pure" horn as an antidote against such ills as poison, stomach trouble, and epilepsy. Drinking cups made from narwahl but erroneously attributed to the unicorn's horn, were common household items. The ancient Chinese considered the unicorn the noblest of animals, Lin, the "powerful one," endowed with majesty and the perfect good.[6] The Church incorporated the animal's benevolent nature into its service as a representative of moral purity and of Christ's having raised the horn of salvation for the world (Luke 1:69). The horn, which ancients had feared as a sword, now symbolized Christ's unity with the Father.

For Don Pedro, however, there can be no cure or ascension to the Father or the Son at the end of the poem. On the contrary, he is assigned to the depths. The last lines based in part on the ambivalence of the unicorn, complete the *burla* (and the ambivalence, of course, reinforces the ironic treatment of the legend). The originally heroic knight has passed through comic configuration to become an undignified object of ridicule. Association with the cosmos, represented by the moon, is replaced by immersion in the depths of the lagoon, where the moon's reflection mockingly appears. His death leads to a place in the slime, among the frogs. The unicorn, symbol of curative powers and salvation, has no recourse but to break its horn. It is powerless when Don Pedro's death is depicted as some type of game ("*jugando* con las ranas," italics mine); and the fabled animal, endowed with magical powers throughout its long history, is defeated in the *Romancero gitano* by a mere *burla*.

Pedro Salinas has observed that ". . .the poetic kingdom of Lorca. . .is under the rule of a unique, unchallenged power: Death."[7] That trait is especially true in the *Romancero gitano*, the mythical intent of which requires the portrayal of a primitive, menacing natural world. Lorca makes it abundantly clear that the powers that lurked in the gypsies' primeval world also appear in the twentieth century, since their struggle against modern society is but a continuation of their timeless battle against life and death. Thus, it often seems in the poems that every element in nature is a threat to human life, be it the moon, wind, water, an animal or a bird, or the most unpredictable of all natural creatures, the human being.

The three symbols that have been discussed here not only exemplify that important trait, but also illustrate Lorca's particular care in effecting the main sociological message of the *Romancero gitano*, the creation of the myth of the gypsy. All were selected from traditional mythologies to strengthen the mythical quality of the work. The dove was recognized as a nefarious symbol in several eastern Mediterranean lands and in later Roman myths. Poorly esteemed in the Old Testament, the dog continued as a representative or harbinger of fatality throughout Europe because of its grieving over graves, mournful baying, or direct connection with dead souls. The unicorn universally lived in fear of death, turned into a hunter, itself, or possessed agents or qualities that could be employed in a struggle to combat death. All these characteristics were of course well known before the writing of the *Romancero gitano*.

Lorca's reliance on traditional material should not, however, obscure the artistry with which he has blended the symbols into his poems. Always an innovator, he states in "Muerto de amor" that dawn will be in the form of a thousand dogs in pursuit of night. In "Thamar y amnón" a Greek goddess's dove, inherited from an Asiatic deity, lies frozen in plural form at the feet of a Biblical princess. The unicorn, which ancients praised for its nobility and beneficial nature, witnesses the death of a Christian knight ingloriously debunked for the first time in literature. Also, a comparison of the dove and the dog with their appearances in other poems reveals interesting thoughts on the part of the poet. Since the dove of "Thamar y Amnón" is counterbalanced by one which signifies the Holy Spirit in "San Gabriel," the contrast seems to be one more example of Lorca's basic belief that life is inherently paradoxical. "La casada infiel" links the dog to a sexual act, indicating that it and death are to be ritually performed in the gypsies' world of nature, as they have been since time immemorial.

Two further conclusions seem in order when terminating a study like this. The previous discussion obviously can only begin to treat Lorca's care in selecting symbols and his artistry in incorporating them into his narratives. But hopefully, it has made clear what a longer study would certainly reinforce. If mythology is to explain a race, the *Romancero gitano* must rank as the world's most outstanding literary evaluation of the Andalusian subculture that Lorca wished to make known to a woefully ignorant world. Finally, a careful reader must note that within this remarkable collection the distant and dim past, the contemporary time of Lorca, and the present day blend into a single unity. That lack of distinction is to make us realize that the *Romancero gitano* transcends the gypsy world of the ballads to issue a most significant universal message: each of us, like the characters in the work, is but one more product of the world of nature, which in the final analysis, is all-powerful, eternal, and supreme. In that respect, Lorca has assured us that until we understand nature's essence fully we really understand nothing; that lesson should not be lost on the human family.

James E. Larkins
Wright State University

NOTES

[1] Calvin Cannon (Ed.), *Modern Spanish Poems* (New York: Macmillan, 1965), p. 59; and Roy Campbell, *Lorca: An Appreciation of His Poetry* (New Haven: Yale University Press, 1960), p. 51.

[2] Maurice H. Farbridge, *Studies in Biblical and Semitic Symbolism* (New York: KTAV Publishing House, 1970), p. 79.

[3] Faebridge, pp. 163-171; and Ernest Ingersoll, *Birds in Legend, Fable and Folklore* (New York: Longman, Green and Co., 1923), p. 133.

[4] A detailed study of the poem, to which this paper is indebted, is Doris M. Glasser's "Lorca's 'Burla de Don Pedro a caballo'," *Hispania*, 47,2 (May 1964), pp. 295-301.

[5] Beryl Rowland, *Animals with Human Faces: A Guide to Animal Symbolism* (Knoxville: University of Tennessee Press, 1973), pp. 152-153.

[6] Harold Bayley, *The Lost Language of Symbolism* (New York: Barnes and Noble, 1959), Vol. II. pp. 99-100.

[7] Pedro Salinas, "Lorca and the Poetry of Death," *Hopkins Review*, 5,1 (Fall 1951), p. 5.

CIRCULARITY AND CLOSURE IN LORCA'S TRILOGY

The world of nature underlies and animates the poems and plays of Federico García Lorca. Even his ideas about imagination, the making of metaphor and the relation of art to life strain against abstraction and come clothed in images derived from nature, from those "hechos de la realidad más neta y precisa."[1] For example, concepts about poetry become themselves poetic images drawn from natural, often Andalusian, contexts, such as Lorca's depiction of metaphor, its shape and range of power. Metaphor couples things together through a daring "salto ecuestre que da la imaginación," a kind of leap on horseback taken by one's imagination so that two disparate worlds are conjoined into a moving, living whole, much as a rider is joined to his horse.[2] Nature informs the definition of living metaphors— "metáforas vivas." These issues from the conjunction of "forma" and "radio de acción," from a visual, concrete shape and a radius of action, a range of suggestion which radiates out from the center, much as a stone, dropped in water, creates a series of pulsating, concentric rings.[3] Metaphor is seen as a dramatic event, a circular configuration, rooted in nature and stylized into art.

Similarly, imagination is construed not as a far-flung, creative impulse but as a finely honed "aptitud para el descubrimiento," a way of seeing that discloses and defines what was already there but unseen: "La imaginación fija y da vida clara a fragmentos de la realidad invisible donde se mueve el hombre."[4] Yet imagination is always limited by reality, circumscribed by nature: "no se puede imaginar lo que no existe; necesita de objectos, paisajes, números, planetas, y se hacen precisas las relaciones entre ellos dentro de la lógica más pura. No se puede saltar al abismo ni prescindir de los términos reales."[5]

The very process of making a poem evokes a flux of images drawn from the natural, physical world. Lorca visualizes writing a poem as embarking on a nocturnal hunt in a far away wood, where the moon, round like a horn of metal, resounds softly and white deer spring from clearings between tree trunks, where night's edges draw together in response to pervasive whispers and deep, clear waters curl round the reeds.[6] In this imaginary world of nature the poet is not an inventor of free forms but a hunter, a trapper, crouched in the center of things, ready to fling his nets and arrows only at living metaphors which hold in their tenace the "palpitating flesh" of hidden realities. In effect, the process traces a probing, circular spiral, beginning with nature's visible signs and winding inward to apprehend underlying, invisible things. Then, like a diver breaking surface, the poet's eye fixes them in visual, startling shapes so that, though returned to a surface, we have traveled in our perception and are not at all in the same place. Metaphor's "forma" and "radio de acción" mirror this circular journey and become part of the action itself, part of that force moving in nature which closes in upon the characters in the trilogy *Bodas de sangre, Yerma* and *La casa de Bernarda Alba.* The purpose of this essay is to show in these plays how that circle is drawn, both conceptually and metaphorically, and how such a dual closure stems ultimately not from human beings but from the world of nature that has sustained them.

Readily visible in the trilogy is a progression toward austerity which culminates in *La casa de Bernarda Alba.*[7] When viewed as a part of a series of three, each dramatic component—setting, colors, sound, lyric forms, the characters and what they do—all trace an impulse toward convergence, the circular reduction of many to few, of few to two, of two to one conjoined, ambivalent reality, and of this one to none, the annihilation of silence, ironically invoked by Bernarda's last word " ¡Silencio!".[8] Diversity of characters in *Bodas de sangre*—adults and children, male and female, ordinary people and symbolic figures like Death and the Moon—telescopes down through *Yerma* to become fixed in the repetitive, all female cast of *Bernarda Alba.* The range of setting—house, cave, inside, outside, field, forest, mountain—narrows progressively to that utter confinement within Bernarda's four "very white," thick walls. Lyric songs, lullabies, prayers, incantations and conversational exchanges converge toward Bernarda's clipped speech and to the spare, repetitive symbols of heat, horse, cane and cord. Paired opposites fold into a single, perduring reality as sound reverses into silence, colors to whites and blacks, love to hatred, freedom to enclosure, life to death.

Within the trilogy each play configures the same convergence. Thus whole and part reflect each other and in that reflection draw the circle tighter still. The resultant pattern is much like a spiral: smaller circles fitted into larger ones, each converging toward a single deadly point—the knife, the stranglehold, the noose. In turn, these points signal the same convoluted constriction as knives wielded by two men change to encircling hands and these to the noose so that homicide reverses into suicide. Thus the external, visible shape of the trilogy, its "forma," is circular. At work within that shape is a process of convergence, the less visible and more menacing "radio de acción." Here, in the very image "radio de acción," lies the irony fermenting in the marrow of each play. For while each dramatic element pulsates outwardly to relate and combine with others, the ensuing series of interlocking relationships tightens the web, pinning the characters to that single, inevitable point. The radius of action explodes and implodes at the same time, not unlike optical illusions which depict white or black, outer or inner, space or confinement. In effect, the radius of action is always dual, always paired to its oppsoite and thus duplicitous, reflecting in that duplicity the circular ambivalence of nature itself. For the tension between two precipitates the reduction to one, and lying curled within that one is the none, the hole, as Poncia says, "un hoyo en la tierra de la verdad" (1443).

At the outer edge of the radius of action are the traditions and values motivating plot: male dominance, marriage and social class. These concepts form the first circles tending toward closure because, by circumscribing action and the characters' lives, they give rise to other, more specific elements, each working in turn to create a final entrapment within each play and, correspondingly, within the trilogy.

"Las ovejas en el redil y las mujeres en su casa" (1312), Juan says to Yerma, confining her to the house with his spinster sisters standing guard. The proverb depicts the patriarchal structure, the rule of men, their land and money, which becomes the most visible cause for the despair and death of *Bodas de sangre*, *Yerma* and *La casa de Bernarda Alba*. Consider how land ownership and money, "plata," motivate plot. There is the Bridegroom's inheritance versus Leonardo's wretched hut and yoke of oxen: "La plata, que brilla tanto, escupe algunas veces" (1213). Money is a force like fate, commingling with nature and death; note how the Moon's ray, poised like a knife, becomes "plata en la cara de la Novia" (1248). There is Juan's grim preoccupation with money as he hoards goods and sheep versus Victor's grave, easy mobility. There is Angustia's inheritance which promotes her ill-fated engagement to Pepe el Romano versus Adela's poverty, "pan y uvas por toda herencia" (1442). As the purse strings are drawn, so is the noose. Land, money and social class dictate alliances set against instinct, the course of blood, the natural order even as these are rooted in nature itself.[9] Traced out from the beginning is a circular pattern stemming from, and closing with, the world of nature.

Land ownership gives rise to male dominance which intensifies and narrows through the trilogy. The Mother's advice to the Bridegroom spells out the concept, handed down from father to son: "Con tu mujer procura estar cariñoso, y si la notaras infatuada o arisca, hazle una caricia que le produzca un poco de daño, un abrazo fuerte, un mordisco y luego un beso suave. Que ella no pueda disgustarse, pero que sienta que tú eres el macho, el amo, el que manda. Así aprendí de tu padre. Y como no lo tienes, tengo que ser yo la que te enseñe estas fortalezas" (1241). Her words still reflect gentleness toward a wife. They find a cruder, more explicit echo in the incantation of the masked figure in *Yerma*: "En esta romería/el varón siempre manda./Los maridos son toros./El varón siempre manda" (1342). Yet it is Bernarda who, by exemplifying *machismo* most rigorously, closes the concept. Male dominance ultimately turns on her, tracing convolution and inversion as a woman becomes a transgressor against other women and against herself. For by shutting doors and windows on the household Bernarda has locked away her femininity, perceived as a caged, animal lust. "Sarmentosa por calentura de varón" (1448), mutters Poncia, even as Bernarda scorns women who glance at men: "Volver los ojos es buscar el calor de la pana" (1449).

In the trilogy *machismo* sets up defenses and draws lines, expressing a hard-hitting, tight closedness. The Mother speaks of "fortalezas," an image denoting hard, smooth exteriors, dryness and toughness, angular, cutting lines. *Macho* means no softnesses, no cracks or openings, no revelations, and the plays mark how these traits progressively narrow.[10] There is the Mother, impassive and black-robed, suppressing under her shawls ever present griefs, "un grito siempre puesto de pie" (1227). Juan, Yerma's husband, is more tense and guarded. Lean and hard like steel, parched and stiff in speech, he is closed up, curled in on himself, "growing backwards," a flat, literal man who barely confides and cannot imagine. Finally there is Bernarda Alba, whose cane strikes the floor with more cruelty and violence than even the Macho's horn that strikes the Female. Her fists beat upon the daughters as she endeavors to keep things sealed up, assuring no cracks, no protesting female impulses, personified by the errant, dreaming figure of María Josefa.

Machismo takes a predominantly visual shape in the plays, reflecting undercurrents of pride, narcissism and fear. It is configured spatially in settings that confine women, walls of smooth, white, dry, flat stone which show no cracks or joints, no dust, no dirt. In *Bodas de sangre* bereaved women sit facing white walls and nailed windows, resigned to their fate. Resignation gives way to anger as Yerma obsessively cleans Juan's house, "pues cuanto más relumbra la vivienda más arde por dentro" (1304). But for Bernarda cleanliness is more than *honra* or decency. Dirt expresses animality, the fleshliness of the body, the seat and stink of the poor. Reproaching the maid's presence Bernarda snaps: "Los pobres son como los animales; parece como si estuvieran hechos de otras sustancias" (1145). This loathing for the body, entailing a corresponding class hatred, drives the servants to polish floors and scrub windows until their hands bleed.

For the house of Bernarda Alba, ruled by macho ethics, is not one but a series of enclosures, each fitted within the other like chinese boxes or concentric rings.[11] There are the four "very white," thick walls which enclose rooms; rooms enclose cupboards which, figuratively speaking, keep in the daughters— "metidas en alacenas" (1518), says Poncia. At the center is the closet where María Josefa sits, locked up tight with *two turns of the key,* sacking stuffed in her mouth to silence those female longings shut up in the hearts of the women. And like closets and cupboards and rooms servants keep to their place, for this is a house of converging enclosures where spatial limitations dovetail with those of sex and social class. Thus silence is dense, palpable, "umbroso;" it spreads to fill the stage, thickening with reciprocal hatreds and resentments as the mistress chastises the servant, the servant berates the maid and the maid in turn lashes out against the wretched beggar woman, yet all the while cursing Bernarda. Hatred comes full circle.

At work among the daughters is the same treacherous collusion: Adela deceives Angustias, Martirio steals the portrait and lies about Pepe's death, provoking Adela's suicide, all of them collaborate to lock up María Josefa. Oppression thus arises from repetitive modes and actions, forming a circular chain tightening around the women who, as if contaminated by the spreading silence, insidiously duplicate one another until the noose is drawn.

In effect, the chain is a dialectical unity, forged by inverted, antithetical pairs such as male/female, tyrant/slave, mother/daughter, servant/master, animal/human, house/village, inside/outside, marriage/spinsterhood, fertility/barrenness.[12] On the one hand, each pair composes a circle because the halves, initially set in opposition, eventually come to resemble each other: servants mimic the master, a house shut down against the village merely duplicates social structures and Yerma's barrenness, setting her apart and against herself, nonetheless does create life, the moving, restless life of the imagination. Out of her longing comes the power to dream and imagine—only Yerma sees the beauty of the weeds, tossing their little yellow flowes in the wind; only Yerma has visions. Women fulfilled in motherhood are little more than archetypes, they are like María whose name— even the moment of conception, visualized as "un palomo de lumbre" (1281)—echoes the Annunciation. But Yerma fills the stage, strong, determined, ironically a "fully rounded" figure. For ultimately the artistic achievement that is the play itself is *Yerma*.[13]

On the other hand, within each pair the halves split, each turning upon ambivalence, engendering contradictory sub-pairs such as movement and stasis, time and no time, sexuality and death. Conjoined opposites thus set in motion a sinister, bifurcating process of reflection and refraction which traces out those concentric rings, one fitted inside the other and all converging to a single point to form a tapering spiral.

The antithetical pair marriage/spinsterhood perhaps best illustrates the process. Marriage promises procreation, fulfillment; spinsterhood means confinement, repression, a wasting away down to death. There are the spinster sisters in Yerma, black-robed and smeared with wax, brooding like leaves that spring over graves, as opposed to the rosy, laughing *lavanderas.* There is Martirio, dry, disfigured, withering with rage, set against Adela, lovely in a green dress. Yet each half of this pair marriage/spinsterhood engenders the same paired themes of sexuality and death. "¿Tú sabes lo que es casarse, criatura?" the Mother asks the Bride. "Un hombre, unos hijos y una pared de dos varas de ancho para lo demás" (1200). Marriage is confinement, the wall: "Miré a tu padre, y cuando lo mataron miré a la pared de enfrente" (1176). The Mother lives within an inner, circular time, turning on past vengeances; she sits, black-robed, with her back to the door and has not been up the street in twenty years.

Everyone, including the Bride, repeats and conforms to this static mode, thus drawing a closed concept even closer. To marry is to gather in one's skirts, live under the wing of the Bridegroom, never leave the house. To marry is to wear black, stiffly starched lace—"encajes duros"—, orange blossoms that "last forever," to look "fixedly" at the Groom, to nail down one's hair with pins. After the wedding two girls squabble over the pins: "Pero los dos alfileres sirven para casarse, ¿verdad?" "Los dos," replies the Bride, grimly (1236). The two pins express the dual nature, the duplicity of marriage, which skewers women to their place even as it pierces and penetrates, opening them to assure the continuance of the race.

For marriage is the wall but also the flowering womb. Even as the Mother defines the fixedness of marriage she exults in the beauty and procreative power of her dead son, "caliente y macho como era" (1199), of her husband, "que me olía a clavel" (1173), men like beautiful flowers, "con su flor en la boca" (1173), men of good blood: "Tu abuelo dejó un hijo en cada esquina. Eso me gusta. Los hombres, hombres; el trigo, trigo" (1174). Everything is, and finds its place, in earth, in nature's ambivalence. Even the engagement present she buys the Bride implies nature's coupling of sexuality and death, for these are "pierced" stockings, embroidered with a swallow on the ankle, a rose on the thigh. Such is a wedding: a blossoming forth but a piercing, a cutting down, a blood wedding. A wedding is a turning wheel, turning as water flows; to the Mother it is like "la roturación de las tierras, la plantación de árboles nuevos" (1240), circular and ritualistic like every event in nature, yet ironic in that very circularity, that repetition that pierces as it fulfills, takes away as it gives. The Mother's own wedding day was like "una herencia" (1240) but her son's wedding leaves her bereft and beggarly: " ¡Tan pobre! Una mujer que no tiene un hijo siquiera que poderse llevar a los labios" (1268).

The duality of marriage draws the circle on the families in *Bodas de sangre*. It narrows further in *Yerma,* where a wife lives trapped in a barren union and a barren body. Finally it closes down upon the house of Bernarda Alba. Marriage and spinsterhood end by reflecting and refracting one another: in *Yerma* a single girl enjoys the same freedom and fulfillment as when married; conversely, the barren wife sits pinned to a chair, just like the spinster sisters. In *La casa de Bernarda Alba* Adelaida, once engaged, must stay behind the door bar, like Martirio the spinster, who blazes in her virginal state. As Amelia advises, married women; worn down by too many children and faced with the wall, lead dismal lives. Even Adela, as Pepe's mistress, could look forward only to the same dependent, slave-like state. Martirio says: "Pero las cosas se repiten. Yo veo que todo es una terrible repetición" (1460). Marriage and spinsterhood stand exposed as a dialectical unity, a single noose drawn tighter by the promise of their apparent contradiction.

The reductive circularity expressed by marriage/spinsterhood surfaces in other, smaller symbolic units such as contrasting motifs, woven into almost every scene so that the process is stylized as an encompassing force like nature's own. Motifs of dryness oppose wetness, harsh sunlight, cool green shade; pinks, blues and soft yellows telescope to whites and blacks, mourning dress is set against colored fans, flowers, the bright skirts of rebellious girls. Stone and steel oppose water and earth, stone and steel being inflexible, sharp, cutting, tools to furrow, grind down, penetrate. The knife cuts with a double edge in *Bodas de sangre;* to Yerma, Juan is rock, wall, "ese muro donde tengo que estrellar mi cabeza" (1334); Bernarda is steely flint, "pedernal"

(1502), a pitiless rod.

Water is set against stone, yet, like other concepts and motifs, water itself engenders the ambivalence of life and death. Nurturing, spilling forth without shape or limit, water can obliterate lines, wash away stones: "Yo, si quiero," affirms Yerma, "puedo ser agua de arroyo que las lleve" (1319). But water turns also on death, depicting at the core nature's paradox and how human beings are trapped in it. In *Bodas de sangre* it chokes, drowns and drags under even as it heals the burnt sores of the Bride. In *Yerma* water takes two symbolic shapes: flowing water versus unspilt, stagnant pools that rot fields and poison people. Juan is a "man made from spit" in contrast to Víctor, whose singing is like a stream filling the mouth, or the fountains and torrents gushing from mountains to signal nature's cleanliness and fecundity. "Los hijos llegan como el agua" (1288), down by rivers, when skirts are drenched in blood and faces are shining. But because Yerma's yearning is meta-physical, reaching beyond nature itself, even flowing water is useless against the stone, the wall.[14] To the old woman who has offered her son Yerma asks: "¿Dónde pones mi honra? El agua no puede volver atrás ni la luna sale al mediodía. . . . Lo mío es dolor que ya no está en las carnes" (1345).

Honra, set within marriage and spinsterhood, is, like water, a principle akin to nature's ruling order.[15] *Honra* also traces out confinements that narrow to the stranglehold and the noose. In *Bodas de sangre* it refers most specifically to virginity and governs the self concept of both Bridegroom and Bride. The Mother declares: "Mi hijo es hermoso. No ha conocido mujer. La honra más limpia que una sábana puesta al sol" (1198). The concept tightens as the play progresses, since for women *honra* is not only beauty or cleanliness but survival. When informed that the Bride has fled with Leonardo the Father cries: "¡No es verdad! ¡Mi hija, no!. . .No será ella. Quizá se haya tirado al aljibe" (1243-44). At the close of the play the Bride herself confronts the Mother, vehemently asserting *honra,* a cleanliness more crucial than even death. *Honra,* not passion, is the root of her will, and she unites with the Mother in the concluding lamentations. But this common lament is not so much reconciliation as convergence, the reduction of two to one. The Bride, previously set in opposition to the Mother, now duplicates her, repeating her lament, absorbing her traditional ways, shrinking to the archtypal, black-robed woman confined within four white walls.

In *Yerma honra* is more apparently a dual concept as chastity becomes explicitly linked to the good name of the house.[16] Thus Yerma stands doubly ringed, oppressed from without and within by *honra,* public opinion, elusive as air, "oscura y débil en los mismos caños de la sangre" (1315), and by her *honra* as a chaste wife. A terrible irony issues from the double ring. Yerma, a rigorously conditioned farm woman, lives so close to nature that she *is* earth, field, "prado de pena" (1316).[17] Accordingly, she seeks fulfillment only within nature's order and the corresponding code of *honra.* But nature, her barren womb, and *honra,* confinement to a barren marriage, block fulfillment. Yerma is denied, walled off from perdurance in children, and so turns her hand against herself, strangling her husband, the only possibility of child, strangling that child, any existence beyond her own flesh. Ultimately she strangles herself.[18] Standing in nature, defined and limited by it, she attempts to use natural means to transcend nature, the tragic aspiration of all symbolic forms, for nature cannot transcend itself—"El agua no puede volver atrás ni la luna sale al mediodía." Homicide loops back as suicide, for Yerma draws the circle on herself: "No os acerquéis, porque he matado a mi hijo, ¡yo misma he matado a mi hijo!" (1350). She prefigures Adela who, from an eagerness to live, must die. Again, in the symbolism of the cord, the tie to life becomes the noose of death. And as if in echo of the Bride's protest Bernarda's only thought is for the dead Adela's *honra:* " ¡Descolgarla! Mi hija ha muerto virgen!" (1532). *Honra* closes the play and, by joining end to beginning, reinforces the circular figure of the trilogy.

The kernel of each play is metaphor, the poet's tool for coupling things together to cage or trap a hidden reality. Each play displays how metaphor is itself an ironic trap, pinching between thumb and forefinger the charactaers who struggle uselessly against their fate.[19] In *Bodas de sangre,* for example, there is the knife which opens the play even as it creates closure by opening the vests of the two men, literally cutting with a double edge. The Bridegroom had called for a "navaja," the broad bladed knife used to hew wood, cut grapes. He saw the knife as an instrument of life, a tool shaping the land, like scythes, sickles and spades. The Mother has cursed these tools as instruments of death, yet she had given the lands to her son, expecting him to cultivate them: "Que caves bien la parte del molinillo, que la tienes descuidada" (1178). Now the Bridegroom has become a wealthy landowner. He can buy the coveted vineyard and marry the Bride. But the wedding, brought about by the richest of cultivated lands, brings only the poorest, most beggarly result—Death, personified appropriately as a beggar crone. To dig around the mill is to dig one's grave; the Bridegroom has worked himself to death. Thus the knife pivots, changing from the broad blade that had promised health and strength to a tiny, glistening fish of steel that kills, "que penetra fino/por las carnes asombradas,/y que se para en el sitio/donde tiembla enmarañada/la oscura raíz del grito" (1272).

Metaphors like the knife as a glistening fish, like the astonished, startled flesh, the dark root of a cry, convey a heightened sensation of life, of a frantic, tangled trembling, felt so keenly because it occurs at the precise moment of death. By making life felt ironically only in death, metaphor mirrors the basic, circular trap of *Bodas de sangre*. The knife images impart specifically this sense of closure, of endings as beginnings, of a fate working through the land and the people because it is a recurrent motif, opening and closing the play; also, visualized at the end as a fish, "sin escamas ni río" (1272), it has become a slippery, animate thing, moving of its own will, independent, as it were, from the men who actually wield it.

This little knife, with neither river nor scales, swims in no channels and so appears everywhere, in fields, tools, plants, in all aspects of nature and human life. Stemming from a common, natural soruce everything meshes; as Vicente Cabrera has said of *La casa de Bernarda Alba*, "details come to be fragments of a perfect mosaic."[20] Each works ominously in the same direction —the pierced stockings, wedding pins, needles to stitch and sew. The Mother views her men as carnations and geraniums, invoking a "floral sexuality," a flowering manhood, only that much more susceptible to being cut down: the son becomes "un brazado de flores secas" (1267).[21] Nature's paradox—sexuality wedded to fatal, cutting edges—is depicted most dramatically in the third act where the Moon, a woodcutter, and Death, a beggar woman, appear on stage. Aching lustfully for the warmth of blood, the Moon collaborates with Death, lighting up the vests of the two men, sensuously fingering the buttons, opening them so the knives will know their way.

In this sequence the knife motif reappears obsessively: the Moon's ray is a "cuchillo abandonado en el aire" (1249), hovering over the two men. He describes how the wind blows hard, "con doble filo" (1251). Leonardo sees the night dying "en el filo de la piedra" (1258), feels glass splinters stuck in his tongue and how the silver pins of the wedding have turned his red blood black. "Clavos de luna" (1260) fuse his waist to the thighs of the Bride, and she would weave a shroud "con los filos de violetas" (1257), sees herself crowned with thorns. Thus metaphor discloses nature's underlying ritual of sexuality and death, duplicated further in the image of the Moon, who seeks another kind of blood wedding, and of Death herself, who contemplates lasciviously, caressingly, the male beauty of the Bridegroom. This is the ultimate trap: the more we live, the more we die. It is expressed not only by the images but by the very concept of metaphor, its "forma" and "radio de acción." The circle is closure. It is also the perfection of art.

Harriet S. Turner
Oberlin College

NOTES

[1] Federico García Lorca, "Imaginación, inspiración, evasión," *Obras Completas* (Madrid: Aguilar, 1963), p. 86. All quotations from Lorca's work are from this edition. Page numbers in the text are given in parentheses. The English rendition of lines from the trilogy are drawn from *Three Tragedies,* trans. James Graham-Luján and Richard L. O'Connell (New York: New Directions, 1955).

[2] Lorca, "La imagen poética de don Luis de Góngora," p. 69.

[3] Lorca, "La imagen poética de don Luis de Góngora," p. 68.

[4] Lorca, "Imaginación, inspiración, evasión," p. 86.

[5] Lorca, "Imaginación, inspiración, evasión," p. 86.

[6] Lorca, "La imagen poética de don Luis de Góngora," p. 74. My rendition.

[7] Francisco García Lorca, "Prologue" to *Three Tragedies,* p. 12.

[8] In a recent article, "Poetic Structure in Lorca's *La casa de Bernarda Alba, Hispania,* 61 (1978), 466-471, Vicente Cabrera takes note of this play's circular structure and traces the symbolic elements used to create that circularity.

[9] According to C. Michael Wells, the norm of nature constitutes reality. See "The Natural Norm in the Plays of F. García Lorca," *Hispanic Review,* 38 (July 1970), 299-313.

[10] For what may be termed a classical description of *machismo,* as exemplified in Mexican culture, see Octavio Paz, *El laberinto de la soledad* (México: Fondo de Cultura Económica, 1959).

[11] By observing how the word "interior" is used repetitively, V.

Cabrera shows how Lorca has created symbolically the "manifold effect of deepness, and suffocating seclusion of the place where the Daughters must live." "Poetic Structure," 469.

[12] Robert G. Harvard comments on the ambivalent symbol in Lorca's *Romancero gitano* in his study "The Symbolic Ambivalence of 'Green' in García Lorca and Dylan Thomas," *The Modern Language Review*, 67 (October 1972), 818. Quoting Harvard, V. Cabrera goes on to explicate the dialectical symbolism in *La casa de Bernarda Alba*, "Poetic Structures," 469-471.

[13] In the ironic ambivalence of barrenness and fecundity may lie one of the reasons for Lorca's predilection for *Yerma*. According to Margarita Xirgu, who played the title role when the play opened in Madrid in December, 1934, Lorca saw himself as the protagonist: "El drama personal de Federico era *Yerma*." From a conversation with Margarita Xirgu, who directed a student production of *Yerma* at Smith College, Northampton, Massachusetts, May, 1967.

[14] Robert E. Lott says: "Her yearning is more than physiological or psychic: it is metaphysical. If it is not satisfied, she will lack authenticity and her world will lack meaning." "*Yerma:* The Tragedy of Unjust Barrenness," *Modern Drama*, 8 (May 1965), 20.

[15] Gustavo Correa, "Honor, Blood and Poetry in *Yerma*," trans. Rupert C. Allen, Jr., *Tulane Drama Review*, 7 (1962), 102.

[16] For an exposition of the two traditional aspects of honor, see Gustavo Correa, "Honor, Blood and Poetry in *Yerma*," 96-110.

[17] For an analysis of Yerma as Mother-Earth, see Patricia L. Sullivan, "The Mythic tragedy of *Yerma*," *Bulletin of Hispanic Studies*, 49 (July 1972), 265-278.

[18] Francisco García Lorca writes: "The instrument which brings death to that child who never existed except in the form of a desperate hope is Yerma herself. The solution, if the term may be so used, she gives out of her own flesh. It is the right thing for the play that Yerma should kill with her own hands and not the knife, as in *Blood Wedding;* those hands held the power of death, embodied now in the central character herself." "Prologue," p. 23.

[19]Several critics have studied the dramatic use of metaphor and symbol in the trilogy. The following articles present particularly detailed explications of imagery: Julian Palley, "Archtypal Symbols in *Bodas de sangre*," *Hispania*, 50 (1967), 74-79; Robert Barnes, "The Fusion of Poetry and Drama in *Blood Wedding*," *Modern Drama*, 21 (February 1960), 395-402; Calvin Cannon, "The Imagery of Lorca's *Yerma*," *Modern Language Quarterly*, 21 (June 1960), 122-130; Vicente Cabrera, "Poetic Structure in *La casa de Bernarda Alba*," 466-471.

[20]Cabrera, 469.

[21]Lorca speaks of Góngora's *Polifemo y Galatea* as having "una sexualidad floral," in "La imagen poética de don Luis de Góngora," p. 80.

THE YES AND THE NO OF LORCA'S OCEAN

Federico García Lorca perceived the idea of synthesis as a poetic imperative. His collected poetry, from 1918 through 1936, sustains an intense dialectic in which life and death are bonded. Whether we examine the provisional modes of *Libro de poemas* or the firm esthetic of *Poeta en Nueva York*, each volume shares with the others a poetics of fusion.

Given the importance of dichotomy as a constant in Lorca's poetry, it would seem fruitful to examine how the poet creates a vision of man and nature based on ambivalence and paradox. Among the natural phenomena which have the highest frequency, *luna, tierra, muerte* and *silencio* are obviously keys in the dialectical play; but other aspects of the natural world remain to be studied in the totality of their poetic contexts.[1] In this paper, I propose a contextual analysis of the motif of the sea in Lorca's poetry, for which more than eighty references attest a phenomenon highly charged with conflictive properties.[2]

The function of synthesis in Lorca's poetic expression is evident from his earliest work. In "Este es el prólogo," which he wrote in 1918, Lorca defined his task pointedly: "ver la vida y la muerte,/la síntesis del mundo,/que en espacios profundos/ se miran y se abrazan" (*Poemas sueltos*, 583).[3]

By observing the process of fusion, one apprehends the overlapping qualities of existence. To put this concept differently, opposition in nature is a superficial perception to be rectified by perspective. Consequently, Lorca ends his "Prologue" in a self-definition:

> El poeta es el médium
> de la Naturaleza
> que explica su grandeza
> por medio de palabras.

If we understand "medium" in its dual sense of intermediary and psychic, this text becomes a blueprint for Lorca's creative achievement.

Libro de poemas

Whatever the stages of development in Lorca's poetry, his first volume belongs integrally with the rest. In thematic content and stylistic features, *Libro de poemas* carries the seeds of conceptual and linguistic innovation. Lorca's treatment of seascape, for example, characterizes his efforts to arrive at a poetic lexicon which would adequately express a protean vision of man and nature.

Lorca's early representations of the sea include the conventional themes of origin, paradise lost, guilt-cleansing and universal paradox.[4] His best verses, however, project the ocean as a dynamic microcosm in which contending forces alternate between affirmation and denial. In its primordial capacity, the sea resonates with harmony; it is like a chamber which may impart secrets to the attentive observer: "La ciencia del silencio frente al cielo estrellado,/la posee la flor y el insecto no más./La ciencia de los cantos por los cantos la tienen/los bosques rumorosos/ y las aguas del mar" ("Los álamos de plata," 268). To regain the wisdom lost, one hones perception to the rhythm of nature: "¡Hay que ser como el árbol/que siempre está rezando,/como el agua del cauce/fija en la eternidad!" (268). A Romantic can reinvent Christianity to make a case for optimism: "El mar es/el Lucifer del azul./El cielo caído/por querer ser la luz" ("Mar," 276). Despite its 'rebellion,' the sea, like man, will be redeemed through love: "La estrella Venus es/la armonía del mundo" (277).

The personification of the sea as original harmony implies a source for recovering poetry, the "canción añeja" which awaits retrieval "muy lejos/del mar y de la tierra." The song is synonymous with the poet's lost innocence, his "alma antigua de niño," consumed by frustration and negative experience ("Balada de la placeta," 251-52). Guilt is also an obstacle to recovering wholeness, and Lorca expresses this cleavage in an affective identification of man and sea: "Mis mares interiores/se quedaron sin playas" ("Manantial," 273). The poet's feelings of sterility are projected by nature, where even silence has been banished. Addressing his invective to a capricious God, the "Yo" compares the exile of silence with a desiccated ocean: "El estruendo remoto/del mar, momificado" ("Elegía del silencio," 219). If God has chosen indifference to the plight of nature ("Si Jehová se ha dormido"), it is the poet who will restore harmony through his artistic will: "vuelve a tu manantial,/donde en la noche eterna,/antes que Dios y el tiempo,/manabas sosegada" (219).[5]

While the foregoing examples of Lorca's early seascapes depend upon conventional referents, "La balada del agua del mar" (263-64) best illustrates his imagistic originality and artistic control: "El mar/sonríe a lo lejos./Dientes de espuma,/labios de cielo." The blending of sky and sea, with the horizon as the space between, suggests beauty and power. Lorca develops this image in a dialogue between a vendor of sea water and the "yo;" each speaker reads the real (agua-mar-sal) or metaphorical language of bitterness (amargura-lágrimas); and each knows that the sea is indifferent to his pain. Unlike the pathetic fallacies which constrain *Libro de poemas,* the impossibility of intercourse between man and ocean gives this poem its poignancy.[6]

Poema del Cante Jondo

Lorca's ability to internalize conflict and to liberate censored drives accounts for the sustained intensity of his second volume. The flamenco genres which he transposes are exploited for their affective vibrancy.[7] One result of Lorca's technique in *Poema del Cante Jondo* is the increased resonance of synthesis; the struggle of opposites will be played more piercingly.

Andalusian geography becomes a metaphor for entrapment and oppression; familiar rivers turn black as they mirror sexual or psychological repression: "El río Guadalquivir/va entre naranjos y olivos./Los dos ríos de Granada/bajan de la nieve al trigo./¡Ay, amor/que se fue y no vino!" ("Baladilla de los tres ríos," 295-96). While the prospect of open waters denotes a way out of the sealed environment ("Para los barcos de vela/Sevilla tiene un camino"), the final images dash all hope of life and love: "Lleva azahar, lleva olivas,/Andalucía, a tus mares" (296).[8] Similarly, the beautiful towers of Seville and Cordoba change into enemy bastions, spewing forth fatal arrows aimed at the multitudes ["La alta marea/de la ciudad" ("Sevilla, Paso," 310)], whose processional is swept unescapably "por el río de la calle,/ ¡hasta el mar!"

Within the confines of human disaster, nature, too, is swallowed: "El bosque centenario/penetra en la ciudad,/pero el bosque está dentro/del mar" ("Palimpsestos," 350), and the city thus confounds enemy forces as if it were a cosmic battlefield: "Hay flechas en el aire/y guerreros que van/perdidos entre ramas/ de coral" (351). For those psyches receptive to its sources, the mysterious tragedy had its announcement in the title, *Cante Jondo:* the art of flamenco communicates the impact of existence shattered. It is the "pena cantando," whose wail has "dejos/de sal marina;" the voice that speaks for everyman, with "algo de mar sin luz/y naranja exprimida" ("Juan Breva," 320). In three separate contexts, Lorca employs variants of the term *ondulante* to signal the all-encompassing threat with which the dance, guitar and voice accompaniment of flamenco vibrate.[9] Thus, he transposes as lyric art the fused genres of flamenco, endowing a static tradition with a peculiarly modern awareness of collective disaster.[10]

Romancero gitano

Despite surface similarities, *Romancero gitano* stands in antithetical relationship to *Poema del Cante Jondo*. Lorca's departure from representation to esthetic personification characterizes the later volume; while both share narrative elements, the condensation of anecdote with lyric clearly distinguishes the form and meaning of the *Gypsy Ballads*. Lorca declared this work, "un libro antiflamenco," and sought to dispel the popular misconception of its derivation from Andalusian reality.[11]

The primacy of myth over narrative is established from the outset: the first two pieces, "Romance de la luna, luna" and "Preciosa y el aire," carry the force of nature unleashed in an uncomprehending universe. For the gypsy girl, this means imminent danger from multiple phenomena: "El silencio sin estrellas,/huyendo del sonsonete,/cae donde el mar bate y canta/su noche llena de peces" (426). Nature's counterpoint becomes the dominant motif, often in complicity with hostile actors. Thus, the pursuite of Preciosa by a sexually aroused "viento-hombrón," is reflected in the enraged ocean ("Frunce su rumor el mar," 427). A parallel clashing of natural forces accompanies the dramatic unfolding of "Muerto de amor," 449-50. Although the narrator cannot locate the source of a crashing sea, its presence foreshadows violent climax: "el mar de los juramentos/resonaba, no sé dónde./Y el cielo daba portazos/al brusco rumor del bosque,/mientras clamaban las luces/en los altos corredores" (450).

Out of radical despair and frustration, personages in *Romancero gitano* become their own antagonists. Soledad Montoya frantically seeks an outlet, only to be consumed by her abiding compulsion: "Soledad de mis pesares,/caballo que se desboca,/al fin encuentra la mar/y se lo tragan las olas" (436). She can no more be shaken from her anguish than the headlong course of suicide diverted; for Soledad, destiny and will are implacably bound: "No me recuerdes el mar,/que la pena negra brota/en las tierras de aceituna/bajo el rumor de las hojas" (437). By this cathexis, she will be 'drowned' whether or not the sea engulfs her longing: there is no reconciliation when death-affirming instincts rule.[12]

Beyond the dialectics which appear to shrink in the encroaching negativities of *Romancero gitano,* Lorca has provided space for liberation and fulfillment. The apotheosis of Antoñito el Camborio, the triumphant beauty in "San Gabriel" and "San Rafael" add an important dimension to the central theme of defeat.[13] In this perspective, the "Romance sonámbulo," perhaps Lorca's most elusive text, may be focused from the angle of its implied wish-fulfillment.[14] On the one hand, the urge for normalcy; on the other, the compelling somnambulistic fantasy. Such an interpretation takes into account the aspirations/illusions suggested in the refrain: "Verde que te quiero verde./Verde viento. Verdes ramas./El barco sobre la mar/y el caballo en la montaña" (430). If we take the second half of the refrain as a yearning for the sea or for nature restored to its equilibrium, other passages in the poem can also be clarified.[15] The somnambulist's projection is filled with negative referents ("soñando en la mar amarga," 430), perhaps drawn from her frustration and anxiety. (The thin narrative line suggests separation from her lover and contraband activities.) The two contradictory perceptions of the sea occur in close textual proximity, and they are symptomatic of the absence of transitions which structures the poem. More importantly, the swing from yes to no, from desire to rejection, speaks for the extraordinary striving of life over death which, I believe, conditions the magnetism of the "Romance sonámbulo" in particular, and Lorca's mastery in general.

Poeta en Nueva York

Having defined his poetic task as the elucidation of synthesis in life and nature, Lorca set for himself a commitment to the gamut of consciousness. While *Poet in New York* may have put this imperative to its most difficult test, the result is a re-inforced affirmation of the potential for survival. Lorca's treatment of the sea-motif during this period demonstrates how he synergised an inferno with a prospect for harmony.[16]

The city which self-destructs concomitantly violates natural cycles. Lorca expresses this disdain for life in a striking image of cosmic détente: "?Cómo fue?/_Una grieta en la mejilla./!Eso es todo!/. . ./Y el mar deja de moverse./_?Cómo, cómo fue?/_Así" ("Asesinato," 490-91). Instead of retaining its dead, the sea vomits up those who sought final rest: "el mar recordó !de pronto!/los nombres de todos sus ahogados" ("Fábula y rueda de los tres amigos," 475). Moreover, the balance of nature has been overcome by pollution and detritus: "el triste mar que mece los cadáveres de las gaviotas" ("Dos odas," 521). Until the course of destruction and oppression has been rectified, the underdogs will not capitulate; they will use their instinctual life-forces to stem the tide: "Aman el azul desierto/ . . ./la danza curva del agua en la orilla" ("Los negros," 477). From their Harlem ghetto, the poet hears the Blacks' crescendo of injustices; as if in response to super-human brethren, he declares their ultimate victory: "tu gran rey desesperado,/cuyas barbas llegan al mar" ("Oda al rey de Harlem," 482).

The world of Walt Whitman is, for Lorca, the antithesis of urban jungle; an epic of the exemplary survivor who holds to his passion for life with unflinching courage. While the rapists and mercenaries pursue their ends, Whitman, the loving outsider, defends vitality and beauty: "ninguno quería ser el río,/ninguno amaba las hojas grandes,/ninguno la lengua azul de la playa" ("Oda a Walt Whitman," 522). Standing apart from those who prostitute life and love, the protagonist's humanity shines uniquely: "Adán de sangre, macho,/hombre solo en el mar, viejo hermoso Walt Whitman" (524). Escaping the degradation around him, Lorca finds in his fellow poet a prospect for re-inventing civilization.

After the assault of barbarity, oases for reflection and recovery give Lorca a pretext for salvaging lost harmony. Poems written after his New York ordeal, retrieve forgotten memories, discover renewal: "Es la niñez del mar y tu silencio/donde los sabios vidrios se quebraban/. . ./Amor, amor, amor, y tu Niñez/del mar" ("Tu infancia en Menton," 475-76). Once he had left the nightmare behind, Lorca sounded a jubilant note of triumph over the forces of annihilation: "Iré a Santiago./Mar de papel y plata de monedas" ("Son de negros en Cuba," 530). Time and distance mitigate the monstrous vision of an alien planet, and a lifetime of perspectivism restores confidence: "Iré a Santiago./El mar ahogado en la arena" (531).[17]

Llanto por Ignacio Sánchez Majías

If Federico García Lorca had not written the greatest elegy in Spanish literature, the author of this paper would have had an easier time of drawing to a conclusion the analysis of ocean synthesis. But the "Llanto" remains an extraordinary document, both within and apart from Hispanic tradition.[18]

It is the absurd gratuity of the bullfighter's death which provokes Lorca's most relentless attack. Since nothing in human or religious terms can encompass this meaninglessness, he composes a dirge to everything: to the planet stripped of impulse and illusion, barren to its fetid core. He refuses to equate Ignacio's death with any precepts or morality, for that would deny the sole remaining impetus to a champion of life's energy: "Vete, Ignacio: No sientas el caliente bramido./Duerme, vuela, reposa: !También se muere el mar!" (544).

No. Our lives are not "los ríos/que van a dar en lar mar,/que es el morir;" rather, to the fifteenth-century poet who composed those lines, to the entire judeo-christian tradition from which they sprang, and to the aggregate of our recreations of his "Lament for the Bullfighter," Federico García Lorca makes his most unyielding demand: live life to its highest pitch and accept even the ocean's nothingness.[19]

Florence L. Yuden
Florida International University

NOTES

[1]The best source for frequency data is Alice M. Pollin's, *A Concordance to the Plays and Poems of Federico García Lorca* (Ithaca: Cornell University Press, 1975). Although this is a paper on the ocean-motif in Lorca's poetry, I do not purport to stem the tide of Lorca bibliography; I list the thematic analyses which I have found most comprehensive: Gustavo Correa, *La poesía mítica de Federico García Lorca* (Eugene: University of Oregon Press, 1957); Cristoph Eich, *Federico García Lorca: Poeta de la intensidad* (Madrid: Gredos, 1958); Carlos Feal Deibe, *Eros y Lorca* (Barcelona: Edhasa, 1973); Jaroslav M. Flys, *El lenguaje poético de Federico García Lorca* (Madrid: Gredos, 1956); C. B. Morris, *A Generation of Spanish Poets, 1920-1936* (Cambridge, University Press, 1969), pp. 1-118; 172-232; Carlos Ramos Gil, *Claves líricas de García Lorca* (Madrid: Aguilar, 1967); Florence L. Yudin, "The Dark Silence in Lorca's Poetry," *García Lorca Review*, VI, No. 2 (Fall, 1978), 151-67.

[2]Number of references: *mar*, 83; *mares*, 12. These data coincide with Pollin, *A Concordance*, pp. 930-31; 1141-42.

[3]All quotations from Lorca's poetry refer to *Obras completas* (Madrid: Aguilar, 1969).

[4]For the basic topoi, see Juan-Eduardo Cirlot, *Diccionario de símboles* (Barcelona: Editorial Labor, 1969), 310; 348-50; Cf. Rupert C. Allen, *The Symbolic World of Federico García Lorca* (Albuquerque: University of New Mexico Press, 1972), "The Ocean-Symbol," pp. 174-87.

[5]For a contrary view of Lorca's representation of God, see Francisco Umbral, *Lorca, poeta maldito* (Madrid: Biblioteca Nueva, 1968), pp. 39-53.

[6]Related contexts of the sea-motif: pp. 178, 192-95, 229, 239, 259.

[7]I am indebted to Correa, *La poesía mítica*, pp. 6-21, and Ramos Gil, *Claves líricas*, pp. 124-41, for their explanations of flamenco.

[8]Cf. "Camino," p. 313.

[9]The images are: *silencio ondulado,* "El silencio," p. 299; *un ondulado desierto,* "Y después," p. 301; *camino ondulante,* "Diálogo del Amargo," p. 337.

[10]I have omitted discussion of the contexts of *mar* in Lorca's third volume, *Canciones,* because the sixteen references repeat motifs we have examined in *Libro de poemas.* Pertinent examples: "La canción del colegial," p. 360; "Fábula," pp. 365-66; "Cortaron tres árboles," p. 367; "Adelina de paseo," p. 377; "[Mi niña se fue a la mar]," p. 378; "La luna asoma," p. 393; "Segundo aniversario," p. 397; "En Málaga," p. 401; "[Agua, ?Dónde vas?]," p. 416; "El espejo engañoso," pp. 416-17; "Dos marinos en la orilla," pp. 418-19.

[11]"Entrevistas y declaraciones," in *Obras completas,* p. 1805.

[12]Carlos Ramos Gil, *Claves líricas,* provides a penetrating analysis of existential anguish in this poem and the *Romancero gitano,* pp. 125; 129-41.

[13]Each of these poems contains the sea-motif (pp. 439, 442, 445).

[14]If nothing else, critics who devise a literalistic interpretation of the "Romance sonámbulo" provide comic relief. Carlos Feal Deibe has responded cleverly to one: "García Lorca y el psicoanálisis. Apostillas a unas apoltillas," *Bulletin of Hispanic Studies,* LIV (1977), 311-14.

[15]The editor of Lorca's "Entrevistas y declaraciones," sees the entire poem as "la aspiración de Granada que tiene ese anhelo al mar" (p. 1806). Recent biography emphasizes the poet's fear of water: Mildred Adams, *García Lorca: Playwright and Poet* (New York: George **Braziller**, Inc., 1977), pp. 71, 156-57; Antonia Rodrigo, *García Lorca en Cataluña* (Barcelona: Editorial Planeta, 1975), pp. 158-65 (Photo).

[16]This interpretation parallels Betty Jean Craige's excellent study, *Lorca's "Poet in New York." The Fall into Consciousness* (Lexington: The University Press of Kentucky, 1977).

[17]Related contexts: "Iglesia abandonada," p. 483; "Ruina," p. 511; "Huída de Nueva York," p. 527; "Vals en las ramas," p. 429.

[18] The best appraisal of the poem's rank in Spanish literature is Calvin Cannon's "Lorca's 'Llanto por Ignacio Sánchez Mejías' and the Elegiac Tradition," *Hispanic Review,* XXXI (1963), 229-38.

[19] Space does not permit discussion of the sea-motif in "Seis poemas gallegos," *Diván del Tamarit* and *Poemas sueltos.* However, the majority of these texts reiterates earlier referents; I list new components which remain to be examined: "Casida de la mujer tendida," p. 570; "El jardín de las morenas," p. 591; "La gran tristeza," p. 606; "soledad insegura," p. 617; "Oda a Salvador Dalí," pp. 618-22; "La sirena y el carabinero," p. 623.

BERNARDA ALBA: NATURE AS UNNATURAL

Federico García Lorca's profound feeling for Nature is evidenced by his symbolic depiction of the characters who populate *Bodas de sangre* and *Yerma*. Yerma's name binds her to the unfertile soil which her husband successfully cultivates, while, at the same time, he completely disregards his wife's needs and maternal desires. La Madre in *Bodas de sangre* also feels a certain affinity to her natural environs and symbolically represents the cultivated land that has born fruit. The identification with and love for Nature is not so apparent in *La casa de Bernarda Alba*.[1] This play is a rural tragedy without a rural scenario, all action being confined within the white-washed walls of Bernarda Alba's house. The protagonist of the drama sees Nature as an adversary; she is constantly struggling, often successfully, to prevent Nature from taking its course.

After the curtain rises, we are struck almost at once by the starkness of the white walls of Bernarda's house in contrast to the black mourning clothes of the women. The lack of color and the austerity characteristic of the Alba home underline the absence of any natural presence on the scene. Bernarda plans to mourn her husband's death for eight years, during which time, she says: "no ha de entrar en esta casa el viento de la calle. Hacemos cuenta que hemos tapiado con ladrillos puertas y ventanas" (p. 1451). Bernarda wants to keep the outside world—Nature included—from her house, and throughout the play Nature rarely imposes its physical presence upon the scene. Offstage, however, outside of Bernarda's house, life goes on as usual. Allusions to Nature's omnipresence are made time and again. In fact, Bernarda's inability to conform with and dominate Nature—her total denial of human nature and instinctual drives—precipitates the tragedy.

For Bernarda, death is more natural than life. It is an occurrence that should be taken in stride, accepted without question and without affliction. Life is what she cannot accept as natural, because her fear of public disgrace, above all else, always motivates her actions. Due to her relatively better financial situation, Bernarda sees herself as the poor village's self-appointed matriarch. Her "illusion of social superiority drives her to impose her distorted [social] code on the household as if in fulfillment of an obligation to her position. A vicious slanderer in her own right, she lives in mortal fear of the malice and slander of her fellow townswomen."[2] Bernarda's paranoia of "el qué dirán de las gentes" supersedes any sentiment of grief she may possibly feel over her husband's death and Adela's suicide. After the mourners leave her house, she shouts at them from behind closed doors: "¡Andar a vuestras casas a criticar todo lo que habéis visto! ¡Ojalá tardéis muchos años en pasar el arco de mi puerta!" (p. 1450). Bernarda only opens her doors to death. The last time the house had been open to the public was when Bernarda's father died. The next time would most likely be for Adela's funeral. The discovery of her daughter's suicide leaves Bernarda only with the thought of covering up Adela's affair with Pepe. Grief is certainly not one of Bernarda's normal emotions; it is mothered by the fear of outside reaction. In order to make herself less vulnerable to public criticism, Bernarda entombs herself and her family in the dreary fortress and imposes a reign of silence on all. Her first and last words on the stage are the same: "¡Silencio!"

Bernarda's aversion to acting naturally is a direct result of her obsession to obey a strict social code that had been laid down by her male forebearers. The eight years of mourning to be observed in her house will be done simply because: "Así pasó en casa de mi padre y en casa de mi abuelo" (p. 1451). It is only natural, then, that she should continue this tradition. The reign of tyranny Bernarda feels compelled to exercise if order is to be maintained makes her completely inflexible to her daughters' needs. Only on one occasion does she show a maternal instinct. When Angustias complains that Pepe seems distracted and is unwilling to confide in her, Bernarda offers the bride-to-be what she considers as sound advice: "Habla si el habla y míralo cuando te mire. Así no tendrás disgustos" (p. 1513). In short, she tells Angustias not to meddle in her husband's affairs, not to become too involved in his life. Bernarda is a loveless creature and cannot imagine how marriage and love have anything to do with each other. "Eso son cosas de debilidad" (p. 1514) she tells Angustias, for, in her mind, any type of emotion is a display of weakness.

As if in order to compensate for her lack of female understanding, Lorca has endowed Bernarda with several male virtues. One very obvious symbol is the cane Bernarda wields to punctuate her commands. Representative of her authority, the cane is also surely a phallic symbol. Adela recognizes this fact when she tries to render Bernarda impotent by breaking her mother's cane in her one momentary surge to power. Bernarda is undaunted. She replaces one phallic symbol for another, as she grabs a rifle from the wall and rushes out to the corral to shoot Pepe. When her shot fails to disable Pepe, she attributes her poor aim to the fact that, after all, she is only a woman: "No fue culpa mía. Una mujer no sabe apuntar" (p. 1531). This is a most convenient excuse for Bernarda, because, she is well aware that a widow with five unmarried daughters must be more than a woman in order to survive. Her success in horse-breeding is commented upon by Prudencia, who, admiringly, tells her that she is "Bregando como un hombre" (p. 1509), to which Bernarda agrees.

Bernarda's distaste for the natural order of the world is manifest in some of the observations she directs towards the world outside of her domain. In this way, she affirms her presumed superiority over all that surrounds her. In disgust, she tells one of the *plañideras* that "Los pobres son como animales; parece como si estuvieran hechos de otras sustancias" (p. 1445). It is ironic that the very same woman to whom the comment is made should tell Poncia, a moment later, that Bernarda is a "Vieja lagarta recocida!" (p. 1447). After the house has been vacated, Bernarda makes another disparaging remark to La Poncia who complains that the solarium is filthy: "Igual que si hubiese pasado por ella una manada de cabras" (p. 1451). Bernarda is aware, however, of what the natural order of the world should be, for she criticizes the town in which she lives for its lack of natural endowments: "este maldito pueblo sin río; pueblo de pozos, donde siempre se bebe el agua con el miedo de que esté envenenada" (p. 1450).

In opposition to Bernarda we find two creatures who accept

Nature with no equivocation. La Poncia does not close her eyes to what transpires within and without the walls of Bernarda's house. She realizes the importance of fulfilling the most basic human instinctual drives and does not try to subvert them. Bernarda, obsessed with the maintenance of her daughters' honor, goes to great lengths to suppress their sex drives. She gives no credence to such feelings, while La Poncia, on the other hand, relates how many years before she had given her oldest son money to see a prostitute, because "Los hombres necesitan estas cosas" (p. 1486). Poncia's recognition of Nature is often reflected in her manner of speech, characterized by an abundance of proverbs and aphoristic sayings, typical of folk tradition and based upon the observation of Nature. She frequently makes reference to natural imagery in her descriptions or explanations of common events. For example, she depicts the harvesters as "árboles quemados" and refers to one young man as "un muchacho de ojos verdes, apretado como una gavilla de trigo" (p. 1485). Bernarda is ignorant of any folk tradition and does not worry about it in the least. When Adela asks her:

> Madre, ¿por qué cuando se corre una estrella
> o luce un relámpago se dice:
> Santa Bárbara bendita,
> que en el cielo estás escrita
> con papel y agua bendita?   (p. 1516)

Bernarda responds: "Los antiguos sabían muchas cosas que hemos olvidado" (p. 1516). Surely, La Poncia would have been able to give a more plausible explanation, but Bernarda cannot be concerned with such trivia. She is not a child of Nature, like most other Lorcan women; in fact, she tells Adela that it is better not to even think about such things. The only time Bernarda resorts to natural imgery is when she wants to denigrate someone. Upon discovering that Martirio was the culprit who had stolen Pepe's photograph, Bernarda strikes her and calls her a "¡mosca muerta!"; she refers to the poor as animals and equates the townsfolk, in one fell swoop, to a herd of goats.

María Josefa, Bernarda's senile mother, is kept locked up out of sight from any roving eye, because her "insanity" would seem to be a disruption to Bernarda's ordered world. Unlike her daughter who seeks confinement, the old woman wants only to escape to the seashore to marry a handsome young man. Her first appearance on the scene, as Act I ends, strikes a discordant note to the black and white monotony of the set. María Josefa has her head and breast covered with brightly colored flowers and demands her mantilla and pearl necklace so that she may be dressed as a bride. Like Bernarda's daughters, she is a prisoner in the house, but it is her madness that prevents her freedom. Although she has only three brief entrances, María Josefa is an impressive symbol of the future. "As such she voices all the fears and desires which the younger women feel but are afraid to disclose in the presence of Bernarda. Her shouts are their innermost secrets. Further, her escape from the guarded room and her subsequent reincarceration are previews of what will occur later in the drama."[3] María Josefa reappears in the last act, shortly before Adela's tragic suicide, this time holding a lamb she claims is her child. She reiterates her desire to escape to the sea and mocks Bernarda and her daughters in a series of animalesque metaphors. As Robert Lima has noted, the image of the sea plays an important role in the play:

> Both in the reality of Lorca's lie, then, and in the kaleidoscopic world of *La casa de Bernarda Alba,* the sea becomes a source of life, of symbolic rebirth, and the passage way to a freedom from the encumbrances of society. Such are the implications in the old woman's desire to journey to the sea. There, away from the oppression of Bernarda's household she can find a new youth in the spray of the waves. But her hope is frustrated by Martirio who succeeds in locking the grandmother in the house.[4]

At the very moment that María Josefa attempts her escape, Adela has made her freedom from the house to meet her lover in the stable. How significant it is then that María Josefa asks Martirio: "¿Por qué aquí no hay espumas? Aquí no hay más que mantos de luto" (p. 1525). The foam to which she refers is that of the ocean's waves, but symbolically it is the male sperm which is incapable of penetrating the egg-like, white "muros gruesos" of Bernarda's house. The old woman's idea of the natural order of the world is diametrically opposed to Bernarda's. She describes what she wants to Martirio in terms of open spaces that would let the outside world and its inhabitants in. Although she is far past her prime, she vocalizes her desire to fulfill certain primal needs: those which Bernarda unequivocally denies and her granddaughters try to repress. María Josefa puts her finger on the problem at hand when she tells Martirio, who is consumed by jealousy: "Pepe el Romano es un gigante. Todas lo queréis. Pero él os va a devorar porque vosotras sois granos de trigo" (p. 1525). Even in her insanity, though, she realizes that her granddaughters cannot be compared to anything so natural as grains of wheat and thus corrects herself: "No granos de trigo. ¡Ranas sin lengua!" (p. 1525). She reduces Bernarda and her daughters to mutations of Nature: toads without tongues.

Pepe, of course, never appears on the scene, nor do any other males. Bernarda Alba's house is a no-man's land in which entry is permitted only to the female sex. The unnatural absence of men on the stage underlines the subtitle of Lorca's play: "Drama de mujeres en los pueblos de España," and stresses the urgency that the spinster sisters feel to be with men. Outside the confining walls of the house, the world is teeming with men: the men on the patio after the funeral, Pepe el Romano at Angustias' window, and the harvesters returning from a day's labor in the fields. The freedom the men have, to come and go as they please, leads Amelia to declare that "Nacer mujer es el mayor castigo" (p. 1486), and Adela expresses her envy: "Me gustaría segar para ir y venir. Así se olvida lo que nos muerde" (p. 1487). At this point, the women hear the chorus of the harvesters clamoring for the girls of the town to open their doors and windows to them. Bernarda's daughters, however, may only peek out at the virile young men from behind the shuttered windows. Martirio does not join her sisters in peering at the workmen but sits alone in a corner, complaining of the intense heat that nauseates her.

Heat is an important leitmotif that runs throughout the play. On the one hand, it symbolizes the burning sexual desire the sisters feel and try to alleviate through their constant drinking of water. On the other, the heat stands for the repressive atmosphere of Bernarda's house, which becomes all the more stifling because of her prohibition of opening windows and doors and her refusal to allow her daughters to leave the house. Bernarda seems unaffected by the heat. To notice it at all would be a submission to Nature's superior powers over her. In the mourning scene, two of the women comment on the heat:

> Mujer 3ª: Cae el sol como plomo.
> Mujer 1ª: Hace años no he conocido calor igual. (p. 1446)

Bernarda pays no attention to their prattle, her primary concern being to serve the guests the lemonade as soon as possible so that they may leave.

Bernarda's daughters are not so immune to the heat as shown by their frequent mention of the discomfort it causes them. Angustias joyfully tells her sisters: "Afortunadamente, pronto voy a salir de este infierno" (p. 1472). Her sisters, aware that their home is a Hell, pick up on the other meaning of *infierno* and begin to complain of the heat, commenting on their inability to sleep because of it.

Adela feels the heat both physially and psychologically. When La Poncia warns her to bide her time and not chase impetuously after Pepe, Adela tells the maid to mind her own business:

> Es inútil tu consejo. Ya es tarde. No por encima de ti, que eres una criada; por encima de mi madre saltaría para apagarme este fuego que tengo levantado por piernas y boca. (p. 1482)

The fire is her burning passion for Pepe, which she consummates in the last act. When, on her way to meet Pepe, she is seen by La Poncia, Adela explains that she had gotten out of bed to quench her thirst: "Me despertó la sed" (p. 1522). La Poncia does not catch the double meaning of her words.

As the women embroider their hope chest linen, they hear the sounds of the laborers singing their harvest song. Although it is mid-afternoon, the men do not seem to be bothered by the heat. Amelia marvels that "no les importa el calor" (p. 1486). The preceding night, a number of the men had entertained a prostitute in the olive grove, and, unlike Bernarda's daughters, were able to extinguish the fire of their sexual passion. Martirio, perhaps the most repressed of all the sisters, is nauseated by the heat and cannot bear it any longer. "Estoy deseando que llegue noviembre, los días de las lluvias, la escarcha, todo lo que no sea este verano interminable" (p. 1488), she cries, but Amelia reminds her: "Ya pasará y volverá otra vez" (p. 1488), intimating the cyclical nature of life in Benarda's house, a situation from which escape is very nearly impossible.

The image of heat acquires its strongest significance in the final act of *La casa de Bernarda Alba*. During the evening meal, at which Prudencia is a guest, the dinner conversation is interrupted by the commotion caused by a breeding stallion Bernarda has locked up in the stable. The stallion tries to break loose by kicking down the walls that obstruct his attempt to mate with the mares. Bernarda orders an unseen stable boy to set the stud free in the corral with the added precaution that the mares be locked up in the stable, out of the stallion's reach. In a low voice she tells Prudencia: "Debe tener calor" (p. 1508). It is not at all surprising that, at this moment, Adela should rise from the table and announce that she is going to get a glass of water. The stallion's struggle to free himself reminds Adela of her own dilemma, and she tries to quench her passion in the only manner permissable in Bernarda's house. The horse is a symbol that appears frequently in García Lorca's plays and poetry and represents "man's hurtling journey through life into death."[5] In the context of *La casa de Bernarda Alba,* the horse not only foreshadows the impending disaster, but, in the explanation of one critic, it embodies:

> . . .the bridled passions which torment Bernarda's daughters. Because the horse is prevented from mating, he tries to break down the walls of his corral; similarly the women, prevented from fulfilling their natural desires to be married, try to break out of their prison. The symbol is clear and obvious. But its second purpose, the ironic, is not as evident. The stallion will have satisfaction in the morning while its human counterparts, particularly Adela, cannot expect such consideration.[6]

In this instance, Bernarda is successful in her domination of Nature. She controls the sexual passions of this animal in the same way she does with her daughters. Her justification for doing so, in this case, is the financial gain that the horse-breeding will return her. Likewise, Bernarda only sanctions Angustias' betrothal to Pepe, because it is a good match. She destroyed the relationship between Martirio and Enrique Humanás, because this suitor did not meet her social standards.

The stallion is also clearly a symbol of the male virility Pepe el Romano possesses and Adela desires.[7] On the final evening of her life, Adela admires the stud, whose whiteness fills the empty darkness of the corral. She tells Amelia: "El caballo garañón estaba en el centro del corral ¡blanco! Doble de grande, llenando todo lo oscuro," and Amelia responds by pointing out the illusory image of the horse: "Es verdad. Daba miedo. Parecía una aparición" (p. 1515). That night Adela, unable to repress her desire any longer, has a rendezvous with Pepe in the stable. When the family is alerted by Martirio's shouts, Adela brazenly tells Angustias that Pepe is now in the corral, "respirando como si fuera león" (p. 1530), thus attributing to him additional "macho" qualities. As if a metamorphosis had occurred, Pepe has displaced the white stallion in the corral—the study desired by all of Bernarda's daughters; the "gigante" alluded to by María Josefa. Just as she had separated the horse from the mares, Bernarda tries to eliminate Pepe from endangering her daughters' chastity. She tries to punish him as she would a disobedient animal and fires a rifle shot at him. Unfortunately, Bernarda's control over human life is not as successful as she would like. She misses Pepe, who will surely boast of his amorous adventures with Adela to the rest of the townsfolk, thus bringing scandal upon the house of Bernarda Alba. Neither will she be able to silence the fact that Adela had taken her own life. Bernarda's desperate attempt to control human nature and the failure to do so successfully is her undoing. Her aversion to letting Nature take its course precipitates the tragedy in *La casa de Bernarda Alba,* for try as she might she is as incapable of suppressing the natural drives of her daughters as she is of keeping Nature from entering her domain. As the curtain falls on the final scene, the hollow echo of Bernarda's "¡silencio!" reverberates on the walls in this house in which life has come to a screeching halt. Without Nature there can only be stagnation and death, old maids dressed in mourning, destined to roam aimlessly through the vacant corridors of Bernarda Alba's house.

Barry E. Weingarten
University of Delaware

NOTES

[1] All quotations appearing in this essay may be found in Federico García Lorca, *Obras completas* (Madrid: Aguilar, 1968).

[2] Sumner M. Greenfield, "Poetry and Stagecraft in *La casa de Bernarda Alba*," *Hispania*, 38 (1955), 457.

[3] Robert Lima, *The Theatre of García Lorca* (New York: Las Americas Publishing Company, 1963), pp. 274-75.

[4] Lima, pp. 284-85.

[5] Lima, p. 283.

[6] Lima, p. 282.

[7] Greenfield shares this opinion. See "Poetry and Stagecraft...," pp. 458-59.

THE VOICE OF NATURE
IN
THE LIFE OF THE WATER

(García Lorca's Vision
from 1923 to 1936)

One of the most beautiful references to nature as a force that influenced the personality of García Lorca since his birth appears in his brother's recollections, *Federico y su Mundo*. Francisco places great importance on the fact that his brother was born in Fuentevaqueros, (note the name of the town) Fuente (Fountain or Source) and Vaqueros (cow-herds or keepers), stressing the significance of the rivers, the water, the storms, and the flash of lightning in one of his brother's early experiences as a child:

> The field was deserted and voiceless. A few heavy drops of rain fell and the wind shook the trees furiously. Suddenly, a dry and formidable crackling, a wild unbriddled horse, out of whose path we had to move, so as not to be trampled, the familiar ozone smell from the rain, and another crackling further away. A pale Federico approached me saying that his cheek was burning and that a blinding spark of lightning had touched him.[1]

Francisco also makes a passing reference to Federico's fascination with his cousin Aurelia's fearful reaction to the summer storms in Fuentevaqueros which becomes more interesting if we remember that one of the last dramatic fragments written by the poet is entitled *Los sueños de mi prima Aurelia*. This is Francisco's version:

> ...Federico, as a child, during the dramatic although infrequent summer storms, used to walk to Tía Frasquita's house, as one would go to the theatre to see a show. Federico used to tell me how cousin Aurelia, half unconscious during a storm, would say,

not without certain theatricality, as she leaned back in her rocking chair: "See how I am dying!"[2]

Francisco and Federico shared the same room and they observed the passing of Halley's comet from the balcony in 1910. . . . Federico was twelve years old.

. . . .

I have insisted upon this aspect of reality as the main source of Lorca's metaphors and poetic images in my previous studies dedicated to *Nature and the Landscape*.[3] Through the study of his language, one discovers a large number of words such as "luna," "agua," "río," "mar," "hierbas," "viento," "caballo," and the names of many flowers and birds which are a constant source of inspiration, persistent through his aesthetic transformation over the years. The nightingale is one of the most subtle and mysterious voices in Lorca's favorite images. One of the things that attracted my attention while reading the dairy by Philip Cummings, *August in Eden. An Hour of Youth* (included in *Songs,* the translation of *Canciones,* 1976), is the charming way in which Cummings describes Lorca's discovery of nature in Vermont and how he fell in love with the plants, the flowers and the fruits in Eden Mills. Cummings remarks that

> The poet meanwhile was making a masterpiece, not in poetry but in floral design. From a simple base of pearly everlastings he added golden sprays of goldenrod and the tall spike of a mullen, a few deep red leaves from a raspberry bush, a bunch of red elderberry and back of this a spray of pine branches, among which he put long stalks of ripe timothy grass. It was a beautiful thing to look at and appeared as a mirror of the Season. The final touch was a group of three small branches with little apples. The poet bore it as his offering to the feast.[4]

The year of the dramatic surrealism of the *Poet in New York* was a revelation of Lorca's inner loyalty to the emotions of his childhood in Fuentevaqueros, and the nostalgic dreams become fused with the new visions of nature in America, including New York, Vermont, Newburg, the Catskills, and Havana. . . A poem entitled "Tu Infancia en Menton," another called "El Niño Stanton," and "Niña ahogada en el Pozo," are related to other poems from his early lyrical works written in his youth. But the two most biographical are, perhaps, the one included in the section called "Poems of Solitude at Columbia University," in which the year of Halley's Comet, 1910, and the parenthesis (Intermission), appear in the title of the poem, dated August, 1929, when Lorca also wrote *Infancia y Muerte, Childhood and Death,* in which we read such poetic confessions as these:

> To find my childhood again ¡Dios mío!
> I ate rotten oranges, old papers, (stable and wheat)
> And I found my own small body eaten by rats (and fish)
> at the bottom of the cistern.[5]

To deal with Nature in Lorca is to deal with his whole poetic world. The poet created his own mythology by selecting the signs from the language of nature. Through the process of aesthetic construction in which he was a very demanding self critic, Lorca mixed the conscious elements with the unconscious sources that had shaped his mind and his sentiments as a man. The first books that he published, *Libro de Poemas* and *Impresiones y Paisajes* are imbued with the magic symbols of the stars, the wind, the sky, the moon, the land with its flowers, trees and birds, the rivers and the sea... Descriptions and tales follow the traditional story teller's style, the fine art of the "juglares" and the creative imagination invested with the richness of musical and pictorial versification. The butterfly of Lorca's first play, as well as *Poema del Cante Jondo, Romancero Gitano* and *Canciones* draw forth his maturity into the realm of poetic wisdom. Nature acquires in each one of these texts a semantic richness, and the poet's language becomes less realistic and more complex in meaning. Nature for Lorca is not only the day and night of life, the contemplation of gardens and landscapes, but human nature as well, the measure of man's dramatic existence. The characters of his plays are in many instances some kind of figures transformed from nature. The horse may be death or sex, or both, and the "weak yellow trill of the canary" ("débil trino amarillo del canario") in a cage, may also be the inner voice of the nun who is embroidering or dreaming, while the flowers and trees, the rose or the orange blossom, may be the cry for motherhood in *Yerma,* while the moon in so many poems is a dream, a nightmare, or a death symbol.

I am interested in sharing with you in this Symposium what Federico called in 1923, the life of the water, *Vida del Agua*. In a letter to Melchor Fernández Almagro, as he explains his involvement with the new poems that he has been writing, there is a moment of deep concentration on this subject:

> I have seen a remarkable book—he says—that remains to be written, and that I would like to write myself. It is about "the thoughts and joys of the water. How many deep and rich wonders can be said about the water! This water poem from my book has opened up inside my soul. I see a great poem of the water, somewhat Oriental, Christian and European; a poem in which the passionate life and martyrdom of the water is sung in ample verses or in vivid syncopated prose. A great life of the water, with very detailed analysis of the concentric circles of its reflection, of the intoxicated music untouched by the silence of the currents. The river and its channels have become part of me. It must now be said that the Guadalquivir or the Miño spring from the source of Fuente Miña and flow into FGL, humble dreamer and child of the water.[6]

The year 1923, when Lorca is a young man of twenty four, is a crucial moment in his development as a poet. André Bellamich, the French critic, refers to this period of intense poetic introspection, as the "etapa meditativa" of Lorca, from 1920 to 1923. The first one to mention Federico in the early 1920's outside Spain, Professor J. B. Trend of Cambridge called him a poet of "Arabia," and from his review of *Libro de Poemas* we gather that Trend was sensitive to the environment of Granada, as he later confirmed in his book on *Lorca and the Spanish Poetic Tradition*[7] when he writes that "García Lorca's corner was a place of trees and falling waters, of dreams, and children playing." At present, Bellamich is putting together the volume of Lorca's *Suites*, variations on such themes as wind, night, gardens, which also includes "Suite del Agua." The first lines are dedicated to a landscape, *País:*

> In the dark waters
> dead trees
> daisies and poppies.

> Three oxen travel
> On the silent road.
> The nightingale,
> heart of the tree,
> In the air...

Bellamich has aleady expressed his opinion about this rare and musical series of *Suites,* suggesting that its composition gives the key to the spirit and the style of what he calls Lorca's "obras negras," such as *Poet in New York, The Public, As Five Years Pass, Diván del Tamarit,* and "almost all of his theatre of frustration."[8]

The most significant myth related to Lorca's obsession with the "life of the water" is Narcissus. The poet goes through the multiple transformations of his introspective lucidity combined with the enigma of his own image reflected in the mirrors created by his mind in the solitude of the Andalusian gardens where he spends most of the time between the years 1920 and 1923. The seeds of frustrated love, the anxiety to create, the death of so many creatures by drowning, the contemplation of stagnant pools, rivers and fountains, the attraction to the wells that reflect the moon and resemble the confinement of a grave, are always reminiscent of Federico's interpretation of the passionate life of the water, its martyrdom, and his own passion to survive the confinement of that "agua que no desemboca," the No-Exit drama of man's life and death.[9]

There is a strong influence in Lorca's personal attitude towards nature that may be traced to the artistic Moorish atmosphere of Granada and the towns of Andalucía where he was raised as a child and where he lived as a young man. The places where he used to spend his leisure time and that he and his family continued to consider "home" even after they had moved to Madrid are all located in the Andalusian region. The way Lorca used to wear the "albornoz" or Moorish cloak in some of the pictures that show his sense of theatrical humor, and his love of beautiful surroundings, music and dance, the observation of details in the decoration of interior settings for his plays and the minute description of Soto de Rojas' "Paradise closed to many, with gardens open to few," attest to the aesthetic roots of a melancholic and mysterious "duende" that Lorca had in his blood and his flesh, so similar to the poetic vein in which Manuel Machado said:

> "tengo el alma de nardo
> del árabe español"

The voice of nature and the life of the water became the hidden leitmotif of Lorca's poetic world through time and space. Bergamín points out that "The poet in New York, once the poet in Granada, remembering his lost Paradise of streams and skies. . . but now alone in a strange city, becomes a child once more; he would scream, if he could, in his inmense, lethal nightmare."[10] Juan Ramón Jiménez, in his sarcastic critical style, once referred to García Lorca as "un alhambrista." This allusion to the precious imagery and the inmersion of the poet in the enchanting atmosphere of the architecture, the gardens, the secrets of the Alhambra, and the sorcery of the "fuentes ocultas," seems to agree with the poet's intention to write a wonderful book on the Life of the Water, as expressed in his letter to Fernández Almagro in 1923. The next thirteen years, until his death in 1936, Lorca wrote poems and plays, lectured on different subjects, visited the United States, Cuba and Argentina, and became the center of attraction of all the new artistic adventures in two continents. The life of the water that he had foreseen as a great Oriental, Christian and European poem is the mythology of his poetic world, in which we discover invisible forms and shadows, the concentric rhythm of the currents that are heard but not seen, and we try to penetrate the mystery of those drops of water "que estremecen las cuevas oscuras," and the reason why the horse of the cradle song in *Blood Wedding* does not drink the water, or why he is obsessed with "una rueca cubierta de arañas y en el lago no canta ni una rana. . ."[11]

García Lorca's poetry and prose and his originality as a lecturer and a dramatist are very enchanting to the ear and the senses, even if the reader or the listener can not understand its meaning or its message. Lorca is a sort of magician who changes the objects into flowers and birds, and a "zahorí" who hears what nobody else is capable of hearing: the water that runs deep underground, the sounds that are in the guitar before it is played, the voice of nature in the life of the water. . .*Diván del Tamarit* is a wonderful statement of how the poet was able to attain a beautiful and sophisticated level of refined obscurity by transforming words of common use, perfectly easy to understand as such, into images of subtle poetic meaning. In one of the poems of this book, "Casida del Herido por el Agua," there is a reflection on the life of the water that he had envisoned. At this moment of his life, the poet is, unknowingly, finishing his work. The year is 1936. Death is awaiting him in Granada. The "Casida" has three divisions, and the voice of the poet is audible as he writes, in the first person singular, what he wants to do and why:

> Quiero bajar al pozo
> quiero subir los muros de Granada,
> para mirar el corazón pasado
> por el punzón oscuro de las aguas.

The desire of the protagonist to search inside and outside, "bajar," "subir," is a measure of the effort to penetrate the unknown, "el corazón pasado/por el punzón oscuro de las aguas." Following the first stanza, the poem describes the drama of the wounded child with a crown of frost and the agony of his own self imprisoned in the water, a pathetic, Narcissistic picture in which one recognizes the repetition of the obsessive vision of Lorca's tragic myth in flesh and spirit.

> The wounded child whimpered
> with a crown of frost.
> Ponds, cisterns and fountains
> Raised their swords to the air.
> Oh, such a fury of love, such a sharp edge,
>   Such a nocturnal murmur,
>   Such a white death!
> What deserts of light were drowning
> the sandy banks of dawn!
> The child was alone
> with the city asleep in his throat.
> A water-spout that rises from dreams
> protects him from the hunger of the algae.

The sequence of exclamations lamenting the fate of the wounded child is a sort of ballad and cradle song:

> !Ay, qué furia de amour, qué hiriente filo,
> qué nocturno rumor, qué muerte blanca!
> Qué desiertos de luz iban hundiendo
> los arenales de la madrugada!

And the transition to a more tranquil voice changes the pace and the rhythm, while García Lorca turns the lyrical key to the visual movement of a ballet, as he had done in the verbal and dancing sequence of the dialogue between the personified figures of the Cascabel and the Pámpano in *The Public*. In the "Casida":

> El niño y su agonía frente a frente
> eran dos verdes lluvias enlazadas.
> El niño se tendía por la tierra
> y su agonía se curvaba.

> The child and his agony face to face
> Were two green rains entwined.
> The child spread out on the ground
> And his agony carved around.

The first line of the opening stanza, "quiero bajar al pozo," is repeated in (I want to descend to the bottom of the well) the fast and moving epitaph at the end of the *Casida:*

> quiero morir mi muerte a bocanadas,
> quiero llenar mi corazón de musgo.
> para ver el herido por el agua.

> I want to die my death by mouthfuls,
> I want to fill my heart with moss,
> To see the wounded one in the water.[12]

Another testimony of nature's presence in the core of his metaphors and symbols appears in the woodcutter who personifies Shakespeare's Moon in the play within the play, *Comedia sin Título*. This Leñador is reminiscent of other characters in his tragedies, a disguised messenger of the unexpected and the supernatural. The role that he plays in *Comedia sin Título* voices the inmortality of poetry in the midst of the revolution that erupts in the theatre. He recites, undaunted by the confusion created by the bullets and the violence in which actors and spectators lose control of their senses and their emotions. His words echo the poet's familiar style:

> Un nardo puede ser estrella o nieve.
> El cielo de la noche, un paño roto.
> Que cante la cigarra o gima el viento
>   lo que importa es el sueño de los ojos.
>
> A tuberose can be a star or snow
> The night sky, a torn cloth.
> Whether the cricket sings or the wind wails
> What matters is the dream of one's eyes

The Leñador goes ahead with his soliloquy, as a madman, with absolute disregard for his safety and a blind faith in his survival:

> El aire es para mí luna de Octubre
>   ni pájaro ni flecha ni suspiro.
>   Los hombres dormirán. Las hierbas mueren.
>   !Sólo vive la plata de mi anillo!
> Tú que estás bajo el agua !sigue siempre!
> Los húmedos *miosotis* tienen frío.
> Aunque la sangre tiña los tejados
>   no manchará la luz de mi vestido.
>
> The air for me is an October moon
> Not a bird nor an arrow nor a sigh.
> Men will fall asleep. The grass dies.
> Only the silver of my ring survives!
> You who are under the water! Forever be!
> Even though blood may dye the tile-roofs
> It will not stain my costume's light.

García Lorca has once again captured the poetic vision of the moon and the water, while the Leñador cries out with a gesture of dismay:

> "It is a beautiful song that perhaps I will not be allowed to sing ever again!"[13]

María Teresa Babín
Professor Emeritus, CUNY

NOTES

[1] Francisco García Lorca. *Federico y su Mundo*. Three fragments published for the first time in *TRECE DE NIEVE* 1-2. Segunda Época, Dic. 1976, p. 11-16, Madrid, España. Número extraordinario en homenaje a Federico García Lorca, que se dedica a la memoria de su hermano Francisco García Lorca. The quotation in Spanish, reads as follows:

> El campo estaba desierto y mudo. Cayeron unos pesados goterones y el viento meneó furiosamente los árboles. De pronto, un tabletazo seco y formidable, un caballo sin silla, desbocado, del que tuvimos que apartarnos para que no nos atropellara, el típico olor de ozono y otro tabletazo más lejano. Federico se me acercó demudado diciendo que la ardía la mejilla y que la había tocado una chispa del rayo, que fue en realidad deslumbrante.

[2] Idem. All translations were done by the author of this paper. Francisco García Lorca read to me the fragment (one act) of the unfinished play *Los Sueños de mi prima Aurelia* when I was doing research in New York, Columbia University, for my doctoral dissertation. The interesting personal explanation quoted in this paper indicates the emotional and psychological impact that Federico was able to transform into a dramatic piece, as he did in so many other instances. The Spanish original of the version given by Francisco, is the following:

> Federico, niño, en los días de las aparatosas aunque pasajeras tormentas de verano, solía encaminarse a casa de la tía Frasquita como el que va a ver un espectáculo. Me contaba Federico que la prima Aurelia, medio desmayada durante una tormenta y no sin cierta teatralidad decía, recostada en una mecedora: !Miren como me muero!

[3] M.T.B. *Nature and the Landscape*. IV, in *El Mundo Poético de FGL*, included in *Estudios Lorquianos*, Editorial Universitaria, Río Piedras, P.R., 1976, pp. 242-290. Mario-Hernández, in "La Muchacha Dorada por la Luna," *Trece de Nieve*, pp. 211-220, makes a beautiful study of this poem.

[4]Philip Cummings. *August in Eden. An Hour of Youth.* In *Songs,* Duquesne University Press, Pittsburgh, 1976, pp. 125-126. There are many pages dedicated to Lorca's visit in 1929. The quotation is on page 160.

[5]Facsímile and Transcription of this poem, by Rafael Martínez Nadal. In *Trece de Nieve,* Dic. 1976, p. 178. See also the notes on the text of the poem, *El viaje: Infancia y Muerte,* by Marína Zambrano, p. 181.

> Para buscar mi infancia! Dios mío!,
> comí naranjas podridas, papeles viejos, (establo y trigo)
> y encontré mi cuerpecito comido por las ratas (y peces)
> en el fondo del algibe. . . .

[6]Letter to Melchor Fernández Almagro. *Obras Completas,* Tomo 11, p. 1063, Aguilar, 1974. The letter includes the chapters and stanzas (prose and verse) that Federico visualizes: Los telares del agua, Mapa del agua, El vado de los sonidos, Meditación del manantial, El remanso. And he adds the idea of writing at the end on the "agua muerta," ¡qué poema más emocionante el de la Alhambra vista como el panteón del agua!"

[7]J. B. Trend. *Lorca and the Spanish Poetic Tradition.* Modern Language Studies. Basil Blackwell, Oxford, 1956, p. 1-22.

[8]André Bellamich. *Sobre un libro casi inédito de Lorca: las Suites.* (Una entrevista imaginaria). In *Trece de Nieve,* Madrid, dic. 1976, pp. 113-116.

[9]Among the poems inspired by the water in Lorca's works, some of the most important are: *Libro de Poemas:* "Lluvia," "Mar," "Meditaciones bajo la Lluvia," "La Balada del Agua del Mar," and "Manantial;" *Canciones:* "Agua, ¿Dónde Vas?", "Mi Niña se fue a la Mar;" *Poema del Cante Jondo:* "Baladilla de los Tres Ríos;" *Poemas Póstumos:* "Canción del Herido por el Agua," "La Suite del Agua;" *Poeta en Nueva York:* "Poema doble del Lago Eden," "Niña Ahogada en el Pozo;" *Seis Poemas Galegos,* Remaxe de Nosa Señora Da Barcá and "Nocturno del adolescente muerto." *Diván del Tamarit* is a fine lyrical monument to the life of the water.

[10]José Bergamín. "Federico García Lorca (La Muerte Vencida)." In: *Poeta en Nueva York,* México, Ed. Séneca, 1940, p. 15-27.

[11]One of the most interesting studies, *Sobre la "Nana del Caballo"* in *Bodas de Sangre* has been written by Ricardo Doménech in *Trece de*

Nieve, dic. 1976, pp. 202-209.

[12]The twelve "Gacelas" and the nine "Casidas" included in *Diván del Tamarit* (1936), as it appears in the last edition of *Obras Completas,* 1, Aguilar, 1973, differ from the former editions of *Obras Completas* (See: Notas al Texto, p. 1383). "Casida del Herido por el Agua" was included in *Poemas Varios,* Vol. VI of *Obras Completas,* Losada, 1940, as "Canción del Herido por el Agua." See M.T.B., *Estudios Lorquianos,* 1976, p. 385.

[13]*Comedia sin Título.* Introducción, transcripción y versión depurada por Marie Laffranque. In: Federico García Lorca. *El Público y Comedia sin título, Dos Obras teatrales póstumas,* Seix Barral, 1978, pp. 273-365.